MW01098839

"Information through Innovation"

Titles available from boyd & fraser publishing company

BASIC Programming
Applesoft BASIC Fundamentals and Style
BASIC Fundamentals and Style
Complete BASIC for the Short Course
QuickBASIC Fundamentals and Style
Structured BASIC Fundamentals and Style for the IBM®
    PC and Compatibles
Structured Microsoft BASIC: Essentials for Business

COBOL Programming
Advanced Structured COBOL: Batch and Interactive
COBOL: Structured Programming Techniques for Solving
    Problems
Comprehensive Structured COBOL
Fundamentals of Structured COBOL

Database
A Guide to SQL, Second Edition
Database Systems: Management and Design, Second
    Edition

Computer Information Systems
Applications Software Programming with Fourth-
    Generation Languages
Data Communications for Business, Second Edition
Ethical Issues in Information Systems
Expert Systems for Business: Concepts and Applications
Investment Management: Decision Support and Expert
    Systems
Management of Information Technology
Pascal Programming for Information Systems
Simple Program Design
Structured Systems Development: Analysis, Design,
    Implementation

Microcomputer Applications
A Guide to Networking
An Introduction to Desktop Publishing
Business Graphics
Contemporary Microcomputer Tools: WordPerfect® 5.0,
    Lotus 1-2-3®, and dBASE III PLUS®
dBASE III PLUS® Programming, Second Edition
DOS: Complete and Simplified
DOS Essentials
Local Area Networking with Novell® Software
Lotus 1-2-3® Quick, Second Edition
Macintosh Productivity Tools
Mastering and Using Lotus 1-2-3®, Release 3
Mastering and Using Lotus 1-2-3®, Version 2.2
Mastering and Using WordPerfect® 5.1
Mastering Lotus 1-2-3®
Microcomputer Applications: A Practical Approach
Microcomputer Applications: Using Small Systems
    Software, Second Edition
Microcomputer Database Management Using dBASE
    III PLUS®, Second Edition
Microcomputer Database Management Using dBASE IV®

Microcomputer Database Management Using R:BASE
    System V®
Microcomputer Productivity Tools
Microcomputer Systems Management and Applications
Microsoft Works: Tutorial and Applications
PC-DOS®/MS-DOS® Simplified, Second Edition
Using Application Software
Using Computers: Lab Manual, Second Edition
Using dBASE III PLUS®
Using Enable®: An Introduction to Integrated Software
Using Enable/OA®
Using Harvard Graphics for Business Presentations
VAX BASIC Programming
Working with Windows 3

Shelly Cashman Series Titles
BASIC Programming for the IBM Personal Computer
Computer Concepts
Computer Concepts with Microcomputer Applications
    (Lotus 1-2-3® and VP-Planner Plus® versions)
Computer Concepts with Microcomputer Applications:
    WordPerfect® 5.0/5.1, Lotus 1-2-3®, and dBASE
    III PLUS®
Computer Fundamentals with Application Software
Essential Computer Concepts
Learning to Use dBASE III PLUS®
Learning to Use dBASE IV®
Learning to Use Lotus 1-2-3®
Learning to Use Lotus 1-2-3® Release 2.2
Learning to Use Microsoft Word® 5.0
Learning to Use SuperCalc®3, dBASE III®, and
    WordStar® 3.3: An Introduction
Learning to Use WordPerfect®
Learning to Use WordPerfect® 5.0/5.1
Learning to Use WordPerfect®, Lotus 1-2-3®, and dBASE
    III PLUS®
Learning to Use WordPerfect®, VP-Planner Plus®, and
    dBASE III PLUS®
Learning to Use WordPerfect® 5.0/5.1, Lotus 1-2-3®, and
    dBASE III PLUS®
Learning to Use WordPerfect® 5.0/5.1, Lotus 1-2-3®
    Release 2.2, and dBASE III PLUS®
Learning to Use WordPerfect® 5.0/5.1, Lotus 1-2-3®, and
    dBASE III PLUS®, Alternate Edition
Learning to Use WordPerfect® 5.0/5.1, Lotus 1-2-3®
    Release 2.2, and dBASE III PLUS®, Alternate Edition
Learning to Use WordStar® 6.0
Learning to Use VP-Planner Plus®
RPG II, RPG III, & RPG/400
Structured COBOL: Flowchart and Pseudocode Editions
Systems Analysis and Design

Software Training and Reference (STAR) Series
dBASE III PLUS®
Lotus 1-2-3®
WordPerfect®

A Guide to Networking

Alan M. Cohen

DataSys Corporation

Boyd & Fraser

boyd & fraser publishing company

Dedication

Many, many, people have helped create this book, and I thank you all from the bottom of my heart. There are four people, however, who are particularly responsible for the creation of the author as he is today, and to whom I dedicate this book:

My mother, Doris, who taught me how to be a good and loving person.

My father, Louis, who teaches me that anything is possible.

My uncle, Harry, who teaches me to believe in myself.

Marian, who helps me move toward these ideals each day.

Credits:

Publisher: Tom Walker
Acquisitions Editor: James H. Edwards
Developmental Editor: Darlene Bordwell
Production Editors: Barbara Worth and Pat Donegan
Director of Production: Becky Herrington
Manufacturing Director: Dean Sherman
Cover Design/Illustration: Michael Broussard
Interior Design/Composition: Rebecca Evans & Associates

Boyd & Fraser

© 1991 by boyd & fraser publishing company
A Division of South-Western Publishing Company
Boston, MA 02116

Library of Congress Cataloging-in-Publication Data

```
Cohen, Alan, 1962-
    Guide to networking / Alan Cohen.
       p.   cm.
    Includes index.
    ISBN 0-87835-554-5 :
    1. Computer networks.   I. Title.
TK5105.5.C56   1991
004.6--dc20                                90-40216
                                              CIP
   2 3 4 5 6 7 8 9 D 4 3 2 1
```

Contents

Introduction

Dallas In the old days (1987), each member of Frito-Lay Inc.'s 10,000-person route sales force had to fill out, by hand, at least two order forms per account—resulting in 100 or more forms for each route. These forms, in turn, were keyed into the snack food giant's mainframe computer system by a team of more than 1,000 data entry operators.

No more. At Frito-Lay, the order pad has gone the way of the dinosaur. Since 1987, Frito-Lay has implemented a computer system that collects, processes, and distributes time-critical data completely by computer.

Each route salesperson is equipped with a hand-held computer for entering order and inventory information. This information is transferred daily via telephone modem to Frito-Lay's central computer system. Up-to-date pricing information is also sent to the hand-held units.

The central mainframe computer system sorts, processes, and distills this cascade of information, presenting it to PCs used by hundreds of Frito-Lay managers. The PCs run EIS (executive information system) software that allows the information to be manipulated in a useful and intuitive graphic format. Managers can also use the EIS system to quickly access route maps, electronic mail, scheduling information, and even the Dow Jones News Service. This information is used to coordinate Frito-Lay's extraordinary complex of thirty-eight plants, which manufacture nearly 100 products in more than 200 package sizes, shipped from more than 1,500 distribution centers.

The results have been excellent. Route salespeople save an estimated hour each day due to the decrease in paperwork and have better control of their routes and cash. Frito-Lay saves an estimated $20 million each year. Executives can spot and respond to snack food trends in as little as forty-eight hours, giving Frito-Lay a crucial edge against the competition.

New York When cashiers at clothing retailer Barney's ring up a sale, they do more than add up numbers. One simple transaction obtains pricing information, performs a credit check, revises inventory records, updates accounting information, collects information on the customer's purchasing patterns for more effective marketing, and of course, adds up the purchases and prints a receipt.

Hanover, N.H. For Dartmouth College students, writing a paper no longer necessarily means trekking across the frozen New Hampshire tundra to the library. Dartmouth has instituted an aggressive policy of bringing computing and communications ability to its students, faculty, and staff. A campus-wide network has been installed, providing a network port in every dormitory room and office.

Among the files available to any of the approximately 6,000 Macintosh computers on the Dartmouth Network are the library's catalog of books, maps, recordings, and serials holdings, the Grolier *Academic American Encyclopedia*, the text of several newspapers, the full text of twenty Shakespearean plays, and the full text of all surviving literature from 800 B.C.E. to C.E. 600.

Electronic mail is also available over the campus network, including the ability to submit homework and papers to professors via the network.

Other facilities include information on job recruiting, housing, dining hall menus, and campus events, and a database of information on Africa and South African investment policies.

These stories are not science fiction, nor are they hopeful predictions by computer salespeople. They are actual examples of how computer communications technology is helping people and organizations to be more productive and effective *today*. Networked computer systems permit groups of people, whether spread over several square feet or across the planet, to share vital information in seconds.

Information about computer networking is typically found in one of three forms:

- Large, technical books aimed at people who will design networking hardware or software from scratch, generally written by and for people with advanced degrees in computer science or related subjects.

- Technical articles in magazines, with obscure tips for professionals in the field of networking.

- "Gee-whiz" magazine articles that tell you what you can do with a microcomputer network in a general sense (share files, share printers), but do not provide hard information on what's involved in implementing, using, and maintaining a computer network.

Many network users, managers, and others who must make decisions regarding the purchase and use of networks and network services need to know the critical aspects of networking without investing years of technical study.

A Guide to Networking is aimed squarely at these people. The purpose of this book is to explain the basics of networking the IBM PC and compatible computers. While *A Guide to Networking* cannot substitute for years of study and experience, it should give you an idea of what is possible with networking—including the benefits, complexities, and pitfalls.

Acknowledgments

The author and publisher would like to thank the following reviewers for their valuable input: Joanne Costello, Massachusetts Institute of Technology; Richard Dempsey, Pennsylvania State University; Irvin Englander, Bentley College; Floyd Leach, University of California at Riverside; Kay Olson, North Hennepin Community College; John Telford, Salem State College; and Coralee Whitcomb, Bentley College.

Communications Concepts

ONE

THE NEED TO COMMUNICATE

Communication has always been important for the survival and betterment of our species. Scientists estimate that a larger part of our brains are devoted to communication than to any other endeavor.

Communication is also critical to the survival of business. Today's business world is *global*, and the ability to quickly process and distribute information to any part of the world can mean the difference between you or your competitor getting the job.

We are familiar with several means of communicating—speech, radio, telephone, television, newspapers, magazines, telegraph, and so forth—all of which have a common goal: to share information. New forms of communication are continually developed to allow more information to spread to more people in less time.

Computer communications is a recent step forward in our quest to spread more information to more people. Computers are extremely powerful tools for collecting, organizing, and analyzing information. Computer communications enables millions of computer users worldwide to share information stored in computers.

Personal computers, also known as **microcomputers**, are the largest and fastest-growing segment of the computer market. The best known personal computers are the IBM PC and its compatibles (hereafter referred to as **PC**s) and the Apple Macintosh family of computers. Because PCs represent the vast majority of installed personal computers, we will concentrate mainly on them. However, virtually all of the concepts and ideas that we will examine are true for the Macintosh—only a few of the specifics differ.

Personal Computers were originally designed as stand-alone, single-user computers. Users soon found that the inability of individual Personal

1

Computers to share information was a handicap. **Local-area networks (LANs)** were developed to allow groups of Personal Computers distributed over a small physical area (e.g., a room or building) to share information and resources. *A Guide To Networking* introduces the theory and applications of Personal Computer LANs.

≡ COMMUNICATIONS MEDIA

When information is communicated, it must be carried by a medium. When we talk to one another face to face, the conversation travels via mechanical vibrations of the air molecules (Figure 1-1a). In this case, the medium consists of the vibrating air molecules.

FIGURE 1-1A

Speech

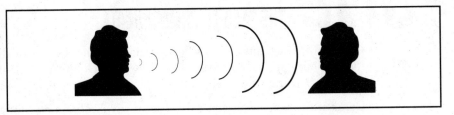

When we read, the medium is the printed page. A telephone is a tool that converts a signal carried by the medium of air into an electronic signal traveling over various cables (another medium), and eventually back into a signal carried by air (Figure 1-1b).

FIGURE 1-1B

Telephone

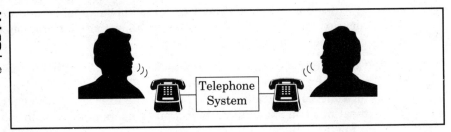

There are three common media for electronic communication: wire, radio, and light.

The Speed of a Medium

One of the most important characteristics of a medium is the amount of information that it can transmit in a given time period. This is sometimes referred to as the speed of the medium. Media described in this chapter are rated by the maximum number of standard single-spaced typed pages that they can transfer each second. We will examine transmission speed in more depth later in this chapter.

Wire

Wire, consisting of thin strands of metal, is the most inexpensive and common way of routing electronic signals. The drawback of using wire is that it is difficult to run over long distances (more than a few hundred meters). Wire is also a relatively slow medium: standard, inexpensive wire is capable of transmitting only a few hundred pages of text each second. Figure 1-2a illustrates the straightforward use of wire.

FIGURE 1-2A

Wire

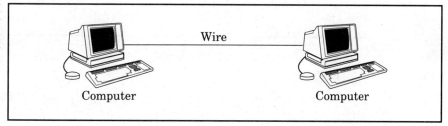

Radio Signals

Radio signals are used to a limited degree for network communications. The most common form of radio network communications uses microwaves, which are very high-frequency signals capable of transmitting a lot of information fast—as quickly as thousands of pages of text per second. Microwaves are scattered or blocked if they strike an object—thus, there must be a clear path between the transmitter and receiver.

Figures 1-2b and 1-2c show two ways in which microwave communications are used: line-of-sight transmission and satellite transmission. Note that satellites generally don't "bounce" the microwave signal: The signal is received and re-broadcast to earth at a different frequency.

FIGURE 1-2B

Radio, line-of sight

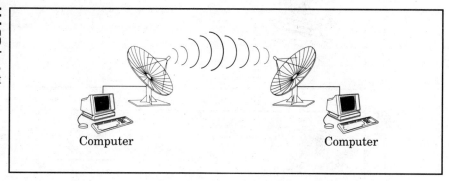

**FIGURE
1-2C**

Radio,
satellite

Light Beams

Computers may also use light beams to communicate. Light beams are similar to microwaves in that they are easily blocked. Light beams are theoretically capable of carrying enormous quantities of information—up to *billions* of pages of text each second. Unfortunately, the communication equipment available today cannot support transfer rates even approaching this figure.

Figures 1-2d and 1-2e show two methods commonly used to transmit light for computer communications. Line-of-sight transmission uses a low-power laser to send information to an optical receiver. Sender and receiver may be up to several miles apart, but the path between them must be free of obstructions.

**FIGURE
1-2D**

Light,
line-of-sight

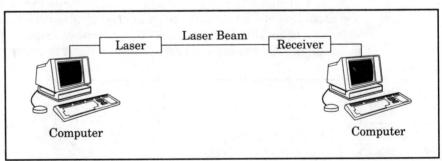

**FIGURE
1-2E**

Light,
optical fiber

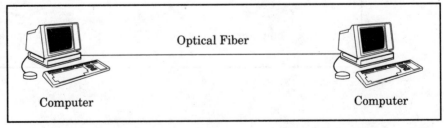

Light communications may also take place over indirect paths by using "light pipes" known as optical fibers. Optical fibers can transmit light over circuitous paths of up to a mile or more.

☰ BROADBAND vs. BASEBAND COMMUNICATION

We are all familiar with the operation of a radio. As we turn the dial to different frequencies, we can listen to different radio stations. While many stations are broadcasting simultaneously, each station is assigned its own distinct frequency: Thus, although the radio receiver is bombarded with a great deal of information (radio stations), it can selectively tune to one station at a time.

Some computer communications systems permit information from several sources to be sent simultaneously, just as we find on the radio airwaves. These are known as **broadband** systems. Broadband systems are a common method of communications between mainframe computers situated in a medium-sized area, such as a college campus.

Computer communications systems that only permit one source at a time to send information are known as **baseband** systems. Baseband systems are less expensive and less complex than broadband systems. Virtually all PC LANs are baseband systems. As we will see later, while baseband systems only permit one piece of information to be sent at a time, they are designed to permit several computer "conversations" to occur simultaneously.

☰ ANALOG vs. DIGITAL COMMUNICATIONS

If we were to measure the voltage on the cable coming from a telephone we would see something like the illustration of Figure 1-3a. If we were to similarly measure the voltage on a cable in a baseband computer communications system, we would see something comparable to Figure 1-3b.

5

FIGURE 1-3A

Analog signal

FIGURE 1-3B

Digital signal

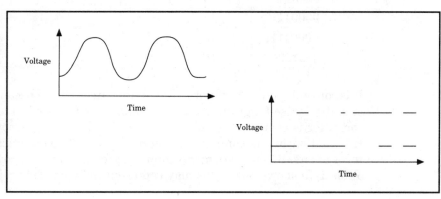

Notice that the signal in Figure 1-3a varies gradually over time: this is an example of an **analog** signal. Analog signals may be at any level at any time.

If we changed the voltage axis of Figure 1-3a to *air pressure*, we would be looking at a representation of the actual soundwave traveling through the air. Thus, human speech is also an analog signal.

By contrast, the signal of Figure 1-3b is always either high or low—or trying to become high or low as fast as it can. This is an example of a **digital** signal. A digital signal may only be in one of two states. The two states are variously known as *high* and *low, 1* and *0*, or *on* and *off*.

TABLE 1-1A

Bytes Representing Decimal
Numbers 0 Through 16

Binary	Decimal
00000000	0
00000001	1
00000010	2
00000011	3
00000100	4
00000101	5
00000110	6
00000111	7
00001000	8
00001001	9
00001010	10
00001011	11
00001100	12
00001101	13
00001110	14
00001111	15
00010000	16

TABLE 1-1B

Bytes Representing Selected
ASCII Characters

Binary	ASCII
00100001	!
00101100	,
00111011	;
01000001	A
01000010	B
01000011	C
01100001	a
01100010	b
01100011	c
01111110	{

It is convenient for computers to communicate digitally because computer circuitry is itself digital. Each of the many thousands of circuits within a computer is either on or off at any time. Each 1 or 0 is known as a **bit**. Information in the computer is represented and communicated by patterns of bits. Bits are commonly found in groups of eight, known as **bytes**. Table 1-1a shows how bytes may represent integers. This representation is known as the binary or base two number system. Table 1-1b shows how bytes can alternately represent some of the alphanumeric characters that may be displayed by a PC. This representation is known as the ASCII code. Bytes may be combined in many ways to represent any sort of information, as long as we all agree on how they are to be interpreted.

Digital signals can be converted to analog by a *digital-to-analog converter* (*DAC*). Likewise, analog signals can be converted to digital using an *analog-to-digital converter* (*ADC*). Figure 1-4 shows how DACs and ADCs can be used to facilitate communications.

FIGURE 1-4

Using analog-to-digital and digital-to-analog converters

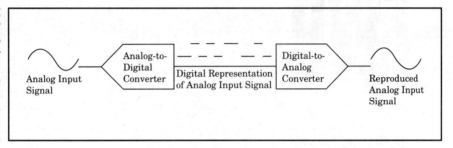

Because computers represent information as bits, and because they communicate by passing bits, it follows that the faster the bits can be transferred, the faster the information can be transferred. The speed with which information can be transferred in a computer communication system is typically measured in bits per second, abbreviated bps.

? How Fast?

One page of single-spaced, word-processed text is equal to about 2,000 bytes of information, or 16,000 bits (8 bits per byte). The text of this book is approximately 200,000 bytes long.

- Old-fashioned (1970's) teletype was transmitted at 110 bps. At that rate, it would take four hours to transmit this book via teletype.

- If we transmitted this book over a typical telephone computer link (2400 bps), it would take approximately eleven minutes.

- If we transmitted this book over a typical LAN (2.5 million bits per second, or mbps), it would take less than one-half of a second.

- If we transmitted this book over a special fiber optic cable-based network (100 mbps), it would take less than one-fiftieth of one second. Looking at it another way, we could send fifty copies of this book in a single second.

7

Sharing Information and Computing Power

TWO

There are two major reasons for linking computer users:

- Sharing information, such as inventory quantities or memos

- Sharing resources, such as printers, plotters, and data storage devices

We can get a better idea of how today's computer systems achieve these ends by looking at how computers have evolved.

≡ THE SINGLE-USER COMPUTER

The first generation of modern (i.e., digital electronic) computers were extremely large and costly. For example, the ENIAC (Electronic Numerical Integrator And Computer) constructed during the mid-1940s is generally recognized as the first modern computer. The ENIAC contained 18,000 vacuum tubes, weighed thirty tons, and required a large team of engineers, scientists, and technicians to keep it operational.

The ENIAC and other computers that followed were capable of solving complex calculations at high speeds, as compared to solving them by hand. Compared to today's computers, however, The ENIAC and its brethren were slow, expensive, large, and failure prone. Due to their great expense, only a few of these first-generation computers were built. There were far more potential computer applications than available computer resources. As a result, optimizing the use of the computer became an important goal.

First generation computers were designed for use by one individual at a time. If you had a difficult numerical problem to be solved, you either waited your turn, or solved it without the computer. When your chance finally came to use the computer, you spent a relatively long time entering the program and data by throwing various switches. Once the program was finally entered, you waited a relatively short time for an answer.

Computer designers soon recognized that this was an inefficient use of the computer's power, because computers spent a lot time waiting for input, and little time doing what they were designed to do: find answers.

☰ BATCH PROCESSING

Batch processing was developed to allow expensive and scarce computers to spend more time computing, and less time waiting for user input. Batch processing made computers available to more users, and less expensive per problem to be solved.

In a batch processing environment, the time-consuming process of program and data entry is physically distinct from the computing process. One or more users may be entering programs and data while a single other program is being processed by the computer.

Users first entered their programs and data on media that could be quickly read by a computer, most commonly a punch card (Figure 2-1). Notice that the punch card contains one line of information, in this case an instruction from a program. Each letter, number, or character on the punch card has a code punched out beneath it, which may be quickly read by the computer. This punch code is said to be machine readable.

FIGURE 2-1

Punch Card

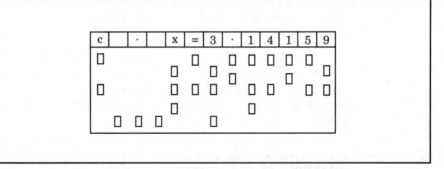

Card punch machines were used to prepare the punch cards. These inexpensive machines (compared to computers) were much like typewriters: as information was typed in at the keyboard, a card was punched. At the end of the line, a new card was automatically started.

A typical computer program might contain hundreds or thousands of lines of instructions and data, and thus might require a large deck of punch cards to completely hold it.

When the user finished punching in the program and data, the card deck was brought to the computer's card reader (Figure 2-2). The entire deck was quickly read at the rate of several hundred cards per minute, and the information processed by the computer. The results were usually sent to a printer.

FIGURE
2-2

Punched
cards and
mainframe

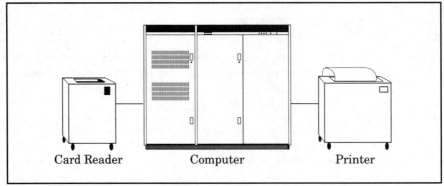

Card Reader   Computer   Printer

In practice, there were usually many card punch machines per computer. Thus, enough users were entering programs at a time so that the computer was always reading cards and processing.

As mentioned before, batch processing was a breakthrough in computing, as it greatly increased the utilization of single-user computers. Computers cost the same to own and operate regardless of whether they are being used for data input or data processing. By maximizing the amount of time they spend computing, batch processing enabled computers to solve many more problems per day, and thus greatly decreased the cost of solving each problem.

Keep in mind, however, that batch processing still permitted only one user at a time to actually use the computer, even though several users could be entering or changing programs at a given time at separate card punch machines.

10

≡ MULTI-USER COMPUTERS

Methods were soon developed that allowed many users to use a single computer at one time. These are referred to as multi-user computers. A diagram of a typical multi-user computer system is shown in Figure 2-3. As can be seen in the diagram, the heart of a multi-user computer system is generally a single large, expensive computer, usually known as a **mainframe**. Many users can access the computer at a time by using **terminals**. Note that **minicomputers** are smaller, less powerful (and less expensive) multi-user computers, but are otherwise identical to mainframes.

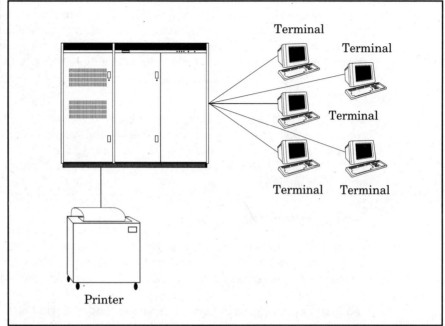

FIGURE 2-3

Multiuser computer

Terminals have no computer power of their own: whatever is typed on their keyboard is sent directly to the mainframe computer. Conversely, anything displayed on the terminal's screen is sent from the mainframe. A typical mainframe may have hundreds of terminals attached to it at a time.

Multi-user computers catalyzed a revolution in computing. Several features of multi-user computers enabled computers to be used for more tasks by more people than ever before.

Decreased Cost Per User

Since many inexpensive terminals could be attached to a single expensive computer, the cost per user was decreased. Let's suppose that a single computer cost $1 million, and a terminal cost $1,000. Prior to the introduction of multi-user computers, giving 200 users simultaneous access to computers would have required 200 computers at a total cost of $200 million dollars, or $1 million per user—an expense greater than most organizations were willing to assume! By contrast, 200 users on a multi-user system would require one computer and 200 terminals, at a cost of $1,200,000, or $6,000 per user. Thus organizations could decrease the cost per user by 99 percent or more by purchasing a multi-user computer.

11

An example of an application made feasible by the cost savings of multi-user computing is word processing. With early single-user computers costing hundreds of dollars per hour to operate, word processing on computers was impractical; it was considerably less costly to simply type documents, even if the documents had to be re-typed several times to correct errors.

The advent of multi-user computers with inexpensive terminals brought computing costs down to the range of tens of dollars per hour, making word processing on a computer cost-effective for many large businesses. Today's PC-based word processors are far cheaper still, and thus are found in almost all businesses.

Real-Time Information Sharing

As multiple users use the computer at the same time, they can share information with each other. And, as the information changes in real time, all users will immediately know, because they share the same base of data. This is known as real-time information sharing. By real time, we mean as the event happens, as opposed to some extended period of time after the event occurs.

For example, let's consider the case where we have several operators taking telephone orders for many products. We would like to be able to tell a customer whether an item they want is in stock. As an item that is in stock, say a madras shirt, is promised to a customer by an order taker, we would like all of the operators to know immediately (i.e., in real time) that the inventory of madras shirts has decreased. This alert prevents operators from promising stock we no longer have. Multi-user computers allow us to share such critical information.

Interactive Processing

One drawback of batch processing was the length of time involved in the computing cycle. After you submitted your deck of cards to be processed, it sat in a line (called a **queue**) waiting for its turn to be processed. It might take hours before the computer reached your deck for processing and printed the results.

With multi-user computers, small tasks could be accomplished in a relatively short time. Thus, answers to problems could be obtained more quickly, usually while you waited at the terminal. Computing became an interactive process: you could sit at a terminal and perform your task in real time.

Let's examine word processing as an example of interactive processing vs. non-interactive processing. The object of word processing is to produce an accurate and visually pleasing document. Word processing today is an interactive process. As we press each key, the computer immediately responds. If that keypress does something unwanted, we immediately see that, and can quickly change it. A non-interactive word processor would be one which accepted say, the text of an entire document punched onto cards along with a group of commands that told the computer how to process and format that document. The computer would follow the instructions and produce the printed document. If a change were to be made, the entire document would have to be re-submitted to the computer.

While non-interactive computing is functional, it is not as nearly as productive (or fun) as interactive computing.

Drawbacks of Multi-User Computers

While multi-user computers were a tremendous advance in state-of-the-art computing, they did (and still do) have drawbacks. The principle disadvantage of multi-user computer systems is that while the computer can support more users, it usually provides less than full power per user. Suppose ten users are simultaneously running large programs that take a long time to complete. A single computer is spreading its power over ten applications: in effect, each application may seem to have only one-tenth of the computer's power available to it. It follows that each application may take up to ten times longer to finish than when run on a single-user computer. As the computer's processing power decreases for each user, users may notice that the computer's response to input is slower. Rather than a smooth interactive process, computing may become sluggish and tedious.

Often this is not quite as bad a problem as it may at first seem. Most common applications, such as word processors and order-entry programs, spend most of their time waiting for user input, rather than doing actual processing. Multi-user computer systems are generally "smart" enough not to waste computer power on applications that are waiting for data. Hence, on a multi-user computer system with 200 users, perhaps only fifteen users are actually processing data at any given moment. Thus, each user would see one-fifteenth of full computer power, rather than the one-two-hundredth that might otherwise be expected.

☰ THE MICROCOMPUTER: RETURN OF THE SINGLE-USER COMPUTER

The groundwork for the microcomputer was laid in 1969 when Dr. Ted Hoff of Intel Corporation designed a programmable integrated circuit for use in calculators. This circuit, the Intel 4004, was the first microprocessor. Prior to the 4004, the "brains" of a computer (Central Processing Unit, or CPU) consisted of thousands of individual components that had to be painstakingly assembled and maintained. The 4004 put the entire CPU into a single component, resulting in a tremendous decrease in cost and increase in reliability. For the first time, the fundamental part of a computer became a commodity item, quickly and cheaply turned out by the tens of thousands.

Electronic hobbyists soon started to use the 4004 and its successors, the 8008 and 8080, to assemble desktop-sized, inexpensive computers, known as microcomputers. The first commercially successful microcomputer, the Altair by MITS, was introduced in 1972. The original Altair was similar to first-generation computers, such as the ENIAC, in that it was a single-user system and had to be programmed directly.

The Altair was *very different* from all previous computers, however, in that it cost less than $500 and easily fit on a desktop. The low purchase price of microcomputers had three basic repercussions that have combined to produce a computer revolution:

- Computers have become accessible to far more users.

- The microcomputer's affordability makes it cost effective for new applications that would be excessively costly on mainframes and minicomputers.

- Microcomputer users tend to have their own computer at their disposal because an entire microcomputer is only slightly more expensive than a terminal.

Although early microcomputers were far less powerful than mainframe computers of that era, the situation has changed dramatically. The power of a typical microcomputer has approximately doubled yearly since 1969, while the power of typical mainframe computers has only increased by a small percentage each year. Today's microcomputers are now used for many tasks previously exclusive to mainframe computers.

Most microcomputers still do not have as much computing power as most mainframe computers. However, a user at a single-user microcomputer often has more power at his or her disposal than a user sharing a mainframe with hundreds of other users. Having such tremendous computer power available for

How Close?

The Gradient Corporation, an environmental consulting firm in Cambridge, Massachusetts, needed to run sophisticated modeling software to fulfill a contract. Based on a few tests, Gradient determined it would take in excess of 20 hours of processing time for the software to run on an IBM 3090 mainframe computer—*at the cost of more than $2,000 per hour.*

Faced with the possibility of spending tens of thousands of dollars, Gradient instead purchased a specially designed PC from DataSys, of Newton, Massachusetts, and software from MicroWay, of Kingston Massachusetts, for a total cost of under $10,000.

The result? The same program was run on the new PC. Processing was completed substantially *faster* on the PC than Gradient's estimates for the 3090 mainframe, and at *far lower cost.*

14

use by a single user has had some interesting consequences: microcomputers can support certain types of software that require too much computer power to run on multi-user mainframe computers. Programs that rely heavily on graphics are particularly slow and unresponsive on multi-user systems.

≡ MULTI-USER MICROCOMPUTERS

As computer users began turning to microcomputers to replace some of the functions of mainframes and minicomputers, they discovered a deficiency of stand-alone microcomputers: data could not be shared. Referring back to our inventory example, each microcomputer in an organization might have had enough power to support an inventory program, but there was no way for one microcomputer to notify the others when inventory decreased due to the filling of an order. This lack of ability to share information among users held back the acceptance of microcomputers for many important business applications that required shared information, such as accounting and databases.

At first glance, the most obvious way to share information among users in a microcomputer-based system would be to use the microcomputer as a multi-user computer by attaching multiple terminals to a central microcomputer. Although multi-user microcomputers are in use today, they represent only a small percentage of microcomputer-based systems. There are two important reasons why multi-user microcomputers are not more popular:

- Although the power of microcomputers has increased tremendously, their price and size have remained small. Because microcomputers have continued to be only slightly more expensive than "dumb" terminals, there has not been much economic pressure to use microcomputers with terminals as multi-user systems.

- Sharing the microcomputer among several users decreases the power available to each user. As previously discussed, certain microcomputer applications virtu-

The End Of The Minicomputer?

NASA, one of the most computer-intensive organizations on the planet, is looking to the new breed of microcomputers based on the Intel 80486 microprocessor to replace its minicomputers.

NASA's Marshall Space Flight Center is replacing it Stellar minicomputers with 80486-based microcomputers. For the price of a single Stellar minicomputer, NASA can provide twenty-five scientists with their own microcomputer.

The bottom line is an immense increase in computing power for the space agency: NASA has documented productivity increases of *30 to 50 times* in a variety of tests using the 80486-based microcomputers.

15

ally require the entire power of a single microcomputer in order to function properly. Thus, these applications cannot function properly in a multi-user microcomputer environment.

Because users wanted to continue to use the powerful microcomputer software they are accustomed to, and because there was not a strong economic benefit in sharing microcomputers via terminals, users needed a method of sharing information among microcomputers rather than a method of sharing a microcomputer among users.

☰ LOCAL COMPUTING/SHARED-RESOURCE MICROCOMPUTER NETWORKS

Figure 2-4 shows an example of a local computing/shared-resource micro-computer network (LC/SR). Each workstation consists of a microcomputer linked to the network, rather than a "dumb" terminal linked to a multi-user computer. These microcomputers are identical to stand-alone micro-computers except that each microcomputer also contains hardware and software that permits it to share network resources (e.g., storage devices, printers, and so forth).

FIGURE 2-4

Local computing /shared resource network

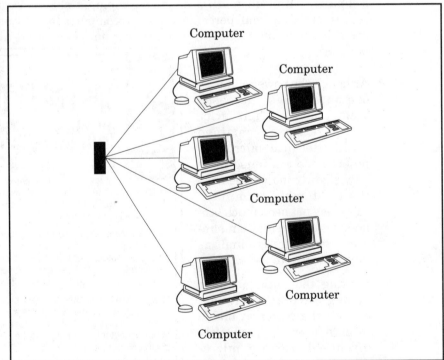

Computer

Computer

Computer

Computer

Computer

Computer

Microcomputers on an LC/SR network operate almost identically to stand-alone microcomputers. The application being used (e.g., word-processing software) is executed by the microcomputer itself, not by the network. The network simply serves as a way of sharing resources (such as printers, data, and software), but *not* computing power. This is in contrast to a multi-user system, such as a minicomputer or mainframe, where resources *and* computing power are shared.

Each of the microcomputers in Figure 2-4 is connected to a **file server**, which is a data storage device (disk drive). Each microcomputer may add or change the information on the file server. As changes are made, they can be accessed immediately by the other networked microcomputers.

The LC/SR network meets our goals:

- Full computer power is available to each user.
- Microcomputers (users) can share information.

Almost all microcomputer networks in use today are of the LC/SR type.

≡ CLIENT/SERVER ARCHITECTURE

The LC/SR network provides us with many of the capabilities of minicomputers and mainframes. There is one situation, however, where the LC/SR network is deficient: sharing very large databases among several users.

Suppose we have a very large database, such as the one maintained by the U.S. Bureau of the Census, stored in a file server on an LC/SR network. Let's further suppose that we need to search the database for all occurrences of the last name *Rambelle*. The data is *stored* in the file server, but the searching is done by the *workstation*, because that is where all of the processing power resides in an LC/SR network. Thus, the entire database, all 250 million or so names, must be sent over the network from file server to database. Even on the fastest network, this transfer will take several minutes to complete. During this time, other network communications may slow down or stop because only one piece of information can be on the network cable at a time. This condition is usually unacceptable.

17

The alternative is the use of special **database servers** to hold large databases. Unlike a file server that is simply a "dumb" shared disk drive, incapable of making decisions about the data it holds, a database server *can* process and make decisions about the data it holds. For example, we could simply ask the database server to count all of the Rambelles in the database and send this number to our microcomputer. Thus, only a single number (the number of *Rambelles*) is sent over the network, rather than all 250 million names of all the people in the United States. Other network communications remain unaffected.

The use of "intelligent" shared resources, such as a database servers, in a network is known as client/server architecture. Their are two major advantages of Client/Server architecture:

- Increase in *speed*. Data moves slowly over network wires compared to the speed at which it moves within a single computer. If the same computer stores the data and sorts through it, the search process can be greatly speeded up.

- *Decrease in network traffic*. As we saw in our example, using an LC/SR network to share very large databases may lead to delays for users because of the high volume of communications on the network. Client/server networks can reduce this traffic significantly, avoiding delays.

Their are two significant disadvantages of Client/Server networks:

- *Cost*. Adding "intelligence" to peripherals can increase their cost.
- *Necessity of rewriting applications*. Much of the software designed for use in stand-alone computers or LC/SR networks must be *rewritten* for use on client/server networks.

In practice, most networks that use database servers also use file servers for more routine operations, such as word processing. In general, client/server operation should only be considered for specific applications, rather than general use. Most applications will not noticeably benefit from client/server operation—but those that do may benefit tremendously.

What Can a Network Do?

THREE

Stand alone, or non-networked, PCs are extremely useful for many tasks, such as word processing, spreadsheet manipulation, and so forth. What are the advantages of connecting these PCs with a LAN?

SHARING INFORMATION (DATA FILES)

As we saw in Chapter 2, networked microcomputers permit important information to be shared among many computer users. The ability to share information in real time among multiple users opens up many applications for microcomputers, particularly business applications.

SHARING PROGRAMS

In an office using multiple non-networked microcomputers, each microcomputer must have a copy of each application program in use. Beyond the obvious expense involved in, say, purchasing fifty-seven copies of a word-processing program, there is the added expense of having to *support* the fifty-seven copies of the program that are floating around. Upgrading to a new version or making a change in the setup requires visiting each of the fifty-seven computers to do the work—a trying task any way you look at it. Also, each user will be inclined to customize his own setup—perhaps radically—making support even more difficult.

A network can bring order to this chaos. A single version of a program can generally be shared by all microcomputers on the network. Having a single central version of the program enables us to *upgrade everyone to a new version by simply upgrading that one copy*—much easier than supporting fifty-seven separate copies!

This approach usually saves money right away: Although you usually cannot pay for only one copy of a program for the entire network, you generally pay full price for the copy to be used on the first microcomputer and a smaller, incremental price for each additional computer on the network.

Suppose a stand-alone version of a program costs $239. The network version costs $349 plus $89 per workstation. At these prices, fifty-seven copies of the program would cost $13,623, while a network version for fifty-seven microcomputers costs $5,422. This would be a substantial savings.

Rather than charging for software on a per-user or per-workstation basis, some software publishers make site licenses available. A site license permits all computers at a particular site or location to use a software program, regardless of number, for a certain fixed fee.

☰ SHARING HARDWARE

Almost universally, businesses are turning to laser printers for production of very high quality documents, ranging from memos to multi-column newsletters. Laser printers are fast, quiet, and expensive, ranging in price from about $1,000 to $25,000. A laser printer can easily print thousands of pages every day, yet no single user is likely to print even 100 pages on a given day.

Given this situation, it makes sense to share laser printers among several users. A network is one way to share laser printers. Networks also allow users to share other expensive peripherals, such as plotters, modems, fax boards, CD-ROMs, and so on.

☰ DISKLESS WORKSTATIONS

Another way to cut costs is to use diskless workstations. In general, hard drives and diskette drives account for approximately one-third of the cost of a microcomputer. Diskless workstations are relatively inexpensive microcomputers. They do not have hard drives, and perhaps not even diskette drives. They rely instead on the shared network hard drive for all data storage. The cost savings of such a system can be substantial in some installations.

☰ SENDING MESSAGES (E-MAIL)

In addition to communicating with a central information source, networks permit communications between network users. **Electronic mail (E-mail)** is a new and exciting application that networks bring to the world of microcomputers: Instead of sending notes and memos on paper, one can send messages and information directly to other users via the network. On some networks, users must check their mailbox for mail. On other networks, mail recipients get messages whenever new mail appears for them. Beyond the obvious advantages of speed of transmission and reduction of paper clutter, there are other conveniences:

- The sender can find out whether the recipient has read the message.

- The receiver can store the messages and search through them at a later date. For example, suppose you were starting a project to determine the effectiveness of a long-running marketing campaign. You could

? How Do LANs Stack Up Against Minicomputers?

In early 1990, *PC Magazine* and Price Waterhouse conducted a test of minicomputers in comparison to PC LANs for accounting applications. The same accounting software was run on both types of computers in a variety of comprehensive tests. The reviewers concluded that, based on current product offerings, *it would require a minicomputer costing more than $1,200,000 to match the performance of a LAN that costs less than $50,000.*

Can LANs beat Minis?, *PC Magazine*, Volume 9 Number 10, P. 195

ask the computer to pull up all memos involved in that campaign for a quick overview of the stages involved in its development.

☰ SECURITY

Security is an important concern in some industries. A single 3.5-inch floppy diskette can hold over 1,000 single-spaced pages of national security secrets, account lists, payroll information, or trade secrets. If confidentiality is important, the use of diskless workstations can be crucial. If the only hard drive and floppy diskette drives in the system are under lock and key, it is much more difficult for torrents of confidential information to flood out the door. Information can be viewed and changed, but not physically removed.

☰ REPLACING MINICOMPUTERS AND MAINFRAMES

Networked PCs can replace existing minicomputer and mainframe systems for certain applications. Some of the advantages that may be realized by switching to networked PCs include:

- Cost savings
- Greater availability of software
- Easier use and maintenance
- Increased performance

21

What Are the Drawbacks of a Network?

FOUR

You rarely get something for nothing. Although networks are extremely useful, their benefits must be considered carefully against their drawbacks.

≡ COST

Network hardware and software cost money. The cost depends on the features of the network and, of course, the number of computers being networked. The cost of a network to link ten microcomputers together may range from $2,500 to more than $35,000. This expense should be weighed carefully against cost savings that the network may yield. For example, a $2,500 network that links ten computers to a laser printer will cost less than purchasing nine more laser printers for $15,000.

≡ ADDITIONAL COMPLEXITY

As mentioned above, networks can decrease the effort needed to support a group of microcomputers. However, networks also bring new complexities to support requirements:

- Users must be trained to use the network properly.

- Support staff must be trained to support the network.

- The network itself is composed of new hardware and software that will add an additional support load.

These complexities can be minimal in practice if the network is designed and implemented properly by experienced personnel. On the other hand, a poorly designed and implemented network can require a tremendous amount of support.

☰ NETWORK DEPENDENCE

When each microcomputer is an island unto itself, the failure of one computer generally means only one user is affected. As users come to depend on a network to share data, printers, and other assets, collectively known as *network resources*, a single failure can mean disruption for everyone on the network, perhaps affecting hundreds or thousands of users. This can be a particularly devastating problem with diskless work-stations, which are *helpless* without the network.

Proper network design can help protect against catastrophe by making network failures easy to isolate and repair.

Fault Tolerance

It is possible to design networks so that they are extremely resistant to breakdowns. This resistance is known as **fault tolerance**.

The basic technique for achieving fault tolerance is to have duplicates of critical network hardware that can take over if the primary hardware fails. For example, we could have a second file server to back up the functions of a primary file server. The two file servers would both receive the same information over the network, ensuring that they both always contain the same information. In the event that the primary server fails, the second server will sense this and immediately take over. Network operation continues uninterrupted while we repair the primary server.

The obvious benefits of fault tolerance are offset by the increased cost of purchasing and maintaining extra hardware. Despite the extra costs, fault tolerance is popular, particularly with organizations that cannot function when the network is not operational, such as banks and hospitals.

Using a Network: The End User's Perspective

FIVE

Whatever the physical changes a network brings (circuit boards, cabling, etc.), the goal of the network is to give the end user important benefits while remaining reasonably invisible. To this end, there are very few new skills that end users must learn—for the most part, the benefits (sharing information and resources) work just as one would expect them to.

Nevertheless, there are several differences the end user must understand when moving from stand-alone to networked microcomputers. We will discuss the common differences in this chapter.

ATTACHING TO THE NETWORK

Under normal circumstances, a networked microcomputer will remain physically attached to the network at all times, even when the computer is turned off. When the computer is turned on, it starts in stand-alone mode. One or more programs must be run to enable the computer to work with the network. This process is known as attaching to the network. There are three common ways to attach to the network:

1. A user may run the program(s) via the keyboard.

2. The computer may automatically run the program(s) upon power-up. The programs are stored on the computer's local hard disk or floppy diskette drives.

3. The computer may automatically run the program(s) upon power-up. The programs are permanently stored in special piece of hardware, known as a boot ROM.

24

≡ NETWORK DRIVES

From the user's point of view, the primary difference between networked and non-networked PCs is the existence of one or more new "hard drives" that may be accessed (e.g., E:, F:, X:, etc.). These new drives are known as network drives because they may be simultaneously shared by all users on the network. Network drives are different from the microcomputer's local drives (generally A:, B:, and C:) in that local drives may be accessed only by that specific microcomputer.

Like local drives, network drives organize files by directories and sub-directories. For all intents and purposes, they *are* local drives, as far as the user is concerned. The procedure for accessing data or programs on a network drive is identical to that for accessing them on a local drive. Suppose a program named PROG was installed on the network drive W:, in the subdirectory \APP. To start PROG, we could type:

W:\APP\PROG

This is also exactly how we would access it from a *local* drive, named W: (if we had one).

≡ SECURITY

Network users must also become accustomed to the security features most networks possess. Although all users *can* share all data, we may not *want* everyone to have access to all data. For example, we might not want most users to have access to files with payroll information. Most networks allow the **network supervisor** (the person in charge of the network) to set up lists of users who may or may not access each directory and file.

To prevent confusion or mischief, we may also allow only certain users to alter or erase information. For example, perhaps only the human re-sources department should be allowed to alter the on-line employee policy manual. Thus, all employees can read the manual at any time, but they cannot add new benefits, such as "unlimited paid leave for employees with sick goldfish."

It may seem most logical at first for the network software to determine access privileges (i.e., the directories and files that could be accessed) based on which workstation (computer) is being used. In that way, the president's computer would be able to access any file, while a salesperson's computer could only access inventory and prices. However, it is better to attach privileges to the *users themselves*, rather than to their computers. In this way the president can access information that she needs from any computer, but no one can use the president's computer to pry into classified information while she is away from her desk.

This situation presents us with a need to indicate to the network who is using which computer at any given moment. The process is known as user **login** (pronounced log in). In order to access network functions, a user must login from the computer he is using, informing the network as to who is using that computer.

Logging in generally consists of telling the network your username (for instance, mine is ACOHEN), and entering a secret password (I'm not telling you mine), which prevents people from logging in under other people's names for whatever reasons.

Before a user logs in to the network, her computer will function using local resources (unless it is a diskless workstation, which cannot do anything without the network). Once the network knows that the user is working on a certain computer, it grants the user access to whichever network directories and files to which that person has privileges.

When the user is finished using a computer, or must step away from it for any reason, the user should **logout**. This tells the network to switch the computer back to local (non-networked) operation until a new user logs in at that location.

☰ SHARING PRINTERS

A network option that users must often get accustomed to is **printer redirection**. On a non-networked computer, printing is generally straightforward: You direct your software to print, and the local printer spits out paper with words and/or pictures.

Printing may be a little more complex on a network, where many printers can be shared. The usual procedure is to enter a command that tells the network, "From now on, send all printing from this workstation to printer X." After this command is issued, printing from that computer will continue to go to printer X until a new printer redirection command is issued or until the user logs off.

Although printer redirection may redirect the print signals to a new printer, it cannot translate between the different formats that must be sent to different printers. For example, if you redirect your word-processing document from your local dot-matrix printer to a network laser printer, you must also tell the word processor that it is now printing to a laser printer, and not to a dot-matrix printer. Failure to do so will usually result in volumes of gibberish spouting from the laser printer.

For this reason, it is a good idea for companies to choose one, two, or three printer standards, and to make certain that all printers purchased adhere to these standards. This will prevent network users from having to choose from a bewildering list of possible printers. Epson, HP LaserJet (PCL), and PostScript are three examples of printer standards that are emulated by many printers.

The Parts
Of a Network

SIX

A network is a complex assemblage of many pieces of hardware and software. The actual pieces used in a given network are dependent on what the network is expected to accomplish: *The first step in designing a network is to establish the number of potential users and their potential applications*. We will examine this planning process in later chapters.

In Figure 6-1 we see the layout of a typical network. Let's take a look at the function of each piece of hardware.

☰ WORKSTATIONS

Workstations are microcomputers employed directly by end users to do work. These are the computers that run applications, such as word processing, spreadsheets, and accounting software. A network may have from one to several thousand workstations.

Each workstation differs from a normal stand-alone personal computer in that it has additional network hardware and software. The hardware, known as the **network interface card** (**NIC**), permits the computer to physically attach to the network cabling. The software, known as the network shell, tells the computer how to use the network to access shared resources, such as disk drives, printers, and modems.

The entire rest of the network (servers, cabling, and so forth) exists merely to support the activities of the workstations.

☰ FILE SERVER

As far as a network user is concerned, a file server is a fancy name for a shared network disk drive. Physically, a file server is a computer with one or more high-capacity hard drives. Most file servers are PCs running

27

**FIGURE
6-1**

Components
of a typical
network

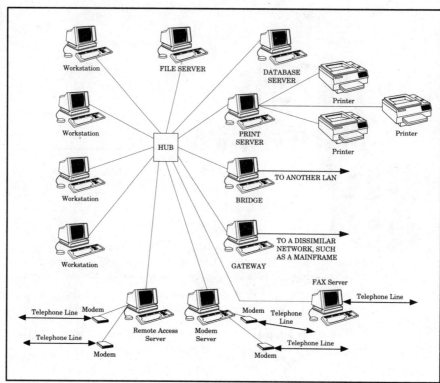

special software to enable them to act as file servers. Minicomputers and mainframes may also act as file servers.

A network may have one or more file servers. In some networks, a PC used as a file server may *only* act as a file server and may not simultaneously be used as a workstation. This is known as a **dedicated** file server. Other networks support a **peer-to-peer resource sharing** system in which workstations can also act as network servers.

☰ DATABASE SERVER

The database server is an extremely exciting component of PC network technology. It can be thought of as a file server that is specialized for use with databases, that is, a special central storage facility for one or more databases. (Some examples of database applications include accounting, inventory, and order entry.)

Until the advent of the database server, minicomputers and mainframes were essentially the only way for large groups of users to simultaneously access the same database. By using database servers, networked PCs can achieve database performance approaching that of mainframe computers in certain applications.

A network may have one or more database servers. They are usually dedicated to their task, and thus are not also used as workstations.

≡ PRINT SERVER

A **print server** is a microcomputer that controls the activities of one or more printers that are shared via the network. A network may have one or more print servers. As with file servers, print servers may be dedicated to that one task or may also be used either as a workstation and/or as a file server, depending on various circumstances.

≡ NETWORK INTERFACE CARD (NIC)

Most PCs cannot connect to the network "as is." That is, a network interface card (NIC) must be installed. The NIC is a printed circuit board that plugs into a slot in the workstation, and as such, is considered a part of the network hardware. Each NIC has one or two special connectors for attaching it to network cabling. Each NIC must conform to the same hardware protocol as the other NICs (i.e., microcomputers) to which it is connected via cabling.

The hardware protocol refers to the physical way that communications take place between network elements. The hardware protocol is transparent to the end user. Examples of hardware protocols include **Ethernet**, **ARCNET**, and **Token Ring**. The features of various hardware protocols are discussed in Chapter 10.

≡ NETWORK OPERATING SYSTEM (NOS)

Network operating system (**NOS**) is the general name given to all of the network software that is directly responsible for networking operations. Every microcomputer that uses or is used by the network will run some sort of network software in conjunction with its regular operating system (almost always MS-DOS or PC-DOS). Novell NetWare is an example of an NOS.

Software that merely utilizes the network, such as word processing software, is not generally referred to as network software, but rather as **application software**.

≡ BRIDGE

A **bridge** is a computer with special software and hardware allowing two or more networks running the *same network operating system* (but often different network hardware) to communicate. For example, a bridge might allow a group of PCs with ARCNET NICs to communicate with a second group of PCs using IBM Token Ring NICs.

Bridge microcomputers can be dedicated to their task or may also serve as workstations or servers, depending on your NOS and other requirements, such as the amount of network traffic and specific protocols to be bridged.

≡ GATEWAY

A **gateway** is a computer with special software and hardware allowing two or more networks running *different network operating systems* (and perhaps different network hardware) to communicate. We would use a gateway, say, to allow PCs running with NetWare NOS to communicate with DEC mainframe computers running the VMS operating system (VMS is both an OS and an NOS).

Gateway microcomputers can be dedicated to their task or may also serve as workstations or servers, again depending on your NOS and other requirements, such as the amount of network traffic and the specific NOS's to be linked.

≡ CABLING

Cabling is simply the wiring connecting the computers in the network. Although installing some wires may seem straightforward, designing the cabling **topology** (configuration) can actually be one of the most challenging and important tasks in designing a network. Cable installation may account for as much as one-half of the cost of the entire network. Network cabling is discussed in more depth in the Chapters 8 and 9.

≡ HUB

A **hub** is simply a device that physically connects cables to each other. IBM has a different name for hubs, preferring to call them **Multistation Access Units** (**MAUs**).

≡ REMOTE ACCESS SERVER

A remote access server permits PCs located anywhere in the world to access the LAN via the telephone. A single remote access server may support one or more remote connections simultaneously.

≡ MODEM SERVER

A modem server permits network users to share modems. These modems may be used to access remote databases and other LANs via telephone lines. Modem servers may simultaneously support one or more shared modems.

≡ FAX SERVER

The telephone facsimile machine (fax) has become an essential part of today's office. Fax machines allow us to send or receive copies of text and pictures to or from any part of the world that has a telephone and a fax machine.

A fax server allows network users to share a fax machine. Computer-based fax machines permit word-processed documents to be sent directly from the computer, without the intermediate steps of printing the document and feeding it to the fax machine. Incoming faxes may be printed to a standard printer. A disadvantage to fax servers is that outgoing documents not generated on the computer must somehow be scanned into the computer.

The Network Operating System

SEVEN

We briefly touched on the role of the Network Operating System (NOS) earlier in this book. Let's now take a closer look at the role of the NOS in tying together a network.

☰ AN INTRODUCTION TO "BLACK BOXES"

If you spend much time around engineering labs, you're bound to run into the term **black box**. In engineering jargon, a black box is a machine that somehow gets a job done without the user knowing *how*. The user only knows how to operate the black box to produce the desired results. Figure 7-1a shows a schematic diagram of a generic black box. Notice that the black box is defined purely by what you can do to it (input) and what the black box does in response (output). We are not concerned with how the black box does what it does—only that it does what we ask of it.

There are many examples of black boxes in our daily lives. To most of us, a television is a black box. We can manipulate the picture and sound with various dials and switches, yet we don't necessarily know how the television works. Figure 7-1b shows an example of the television as a black box.

FIGURE 7-1A

A black box

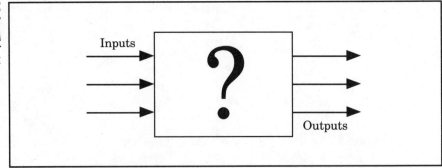

Inputs

?

Outputs

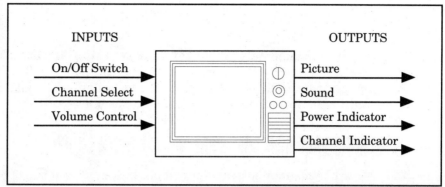

FIGURE 7-1B

A Television as a Black Box

The automobile is another example of a black box. Most of us know how to control an automobile to get where we'd like, yet few of us understand how the symphony of parts under the hood interacts with the controls to get us there.

Let's take a deeper look at the components of a car. It has an engine to provide propulsion. It has a fuel system to provide an energy source to the engine. The steering system controls the car's direction of motion. The drive train transfers the engine's power to the wheels. The suspension system provides a smooth ride to the vehicle's occupants. Figure 7-2 illustrates a view of an automobile as a collection of major sub-assemblies.

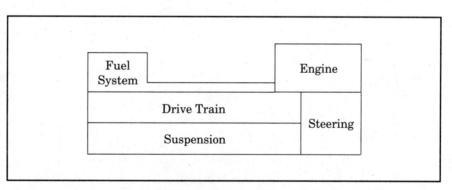

FIGURE 7-2

An automobile as a collection of black boxes

If we think about it, we can conclude that just as the entire automobile can be considered a single black box, each subassembly in the car can be defined as a black box. For example, the engine can be roughly defined as a machine that produces mechanical energy by burning gasoline. The amount of mechanical energy produced at any instant is determined by the amount of fuel being fed to it at that time.

We could continue to define each subassembly as a group of more basic parts. The drive train, for example, comprises a transmission, transmission shaft, U-joints, axles, and a differential. Each of these might in turn be viewed as a black box.

Even a fundamental part of a car, such as a spring, is a black box. We may understand that a spring snaps back when pushed or pulled, but we don't necessarily need to understand the molecular forces and interactions within the spring that cause it to behave as it does.

HARDWARE AND SOFTWARE: A TWO-LAYER MODEL

In a like manner, a computer can be thought of as a single black box, or collection of black boxes. In Figure 7-3a, we see a computer system separated into two black boxes: hardware and software. **Hardware** refers to the physical materials and circuits that constitute the computer. **Software** refers to the instructions that run the computer and tell it what to do.

FIGURE 7-3A

A computer as two black boxes

FIGURE 7-3B

2-layer computer model

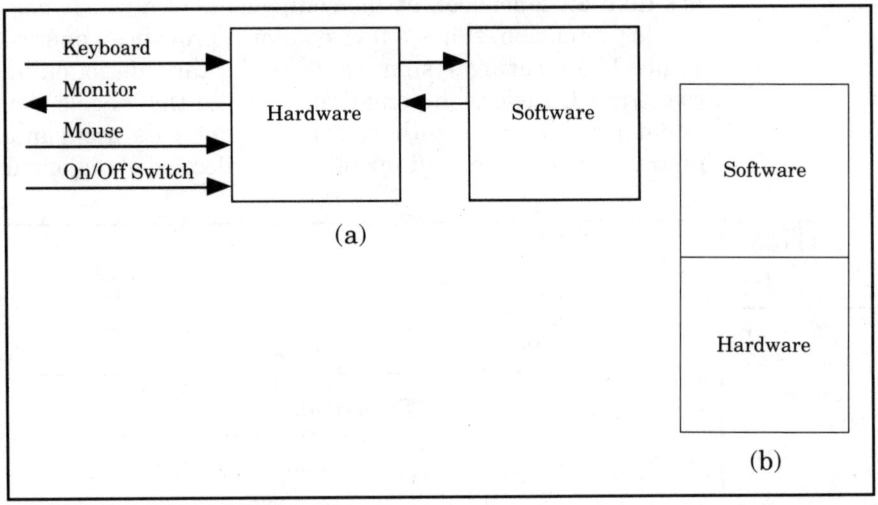

The difference between hardware and software is relatively easy to recognize. When we switch from a word-processing program to a spreadsheet program, the computer does not physically change, at least significantly. What does change is the software, or the set of instructions that tells the hardware how to respond to your input from the keyboard.

Figure 7-3b shows our two black boxes, stacked one atop the other like layers in a cake. This way of depicting a computer is known as a model, and each black box is known as, well, a layer. Figure 7-3b is a model, consisting of two layers, and thus is referred to as a two-layer model of a computer.

☰ THE COMPUTER OPERATING SYSTEM: A THREE-LAYER MODEL

Figure 7-4 shows our computer model broken out into three layers. Note that the hardware layer is the same as that of Figure 7-3b, but the software layer has been further split into two layers: The application software layer and the **operating system (OS)** layer.

FIGURE 7-4

3-layer computer model

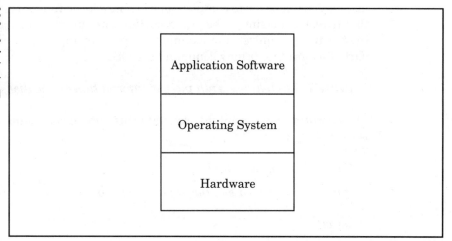

The application software layer is the layer of software with which we are all familiar. Examples of application software are word processing (e.g., WordPerfect) and spreadsheets (e.g., Lotus 1-2-3). Although you are probably familiar with the look and feel of one or more application software products, the operation of the operating system layer is quite subtle.

The OS layer, designed to be invisible to the user, lies between the application software and the hardware. Looking at Figure 7-4, we can see that there is no direct path between the application software and the hardware. When the applications layer needs something from the hardware layer, it first sends the request to the OS layer. The OS forwards the request to the hardware. The hardware performs the desired action and may return some information to the OS, which in turn passes the information to the application.

The operating system serves two purposes: to provide a common set of computer functions, and to provide hardware independence.

Common Computer Functions

There are certain tasks that virtually all application programs must perform. These include:

35

- Getting input from the keyboard
- Reading from and writing to disk drives
- Writing information to the computer screen

Each of these tasks is a basic function as far as the application software is concerned. However, the hardware layer may require many different instructions in order to complete one of these basic functions. It is the OS that translates a simple, basic instruction into the set of instructions that the hardware requires. For example, suppose an application needs to read part of a data file. It may command the OS:

Retrieve the eighty-seventh piece of information on the disk drive F:

The operating system might translate this simple command to the hardware as follows:

Check if disk drive F: exists

If it does not, tell this to the application program

Otherwise

Start up disk drive F:

Find the eighty-seventh piece of data

Read this piece of information

Send information to the application program

Stop disk drive F:

We can see that in this case, the operating system simplifies the basic task of reading a piece of data from a disk drive. The application program need only issue one basic instruction rather than the eight or more that would be necessary without an operating system.

The typical OS contains several hundred functions, each of which are translated to one or more instructions on the hardware side of the layer.

Hardware Independence

Looking back to Figure 7-4, we notice that as far as the application program is concerned, the only other thing that exists in this world is the OS. That is, the application program can only communicate through the OS. Because of this, the OS functions as a buffer between the application and the hardware.

Suppose we design new hardware that can operate much faster than before. Let's further suppose that this new hardware functions differently than the old hardware, requiring different instructions to perform certain tasks.

If OS's did not exist, we would have to rewrite all of our application software to take advantage of the new, faster hardware. Fortunately, because many applications usually share a single OS, we need only redesign the OS layer so that it translates the exact same set of commands on the applications side to the new groups of commands needed on the hardware side. Having an OS layer allows us to design many thousands of applications for a single OS, and use these applications on different types of hardware by simply adapting the OS.

Popular Operating Systems

The most common OS's for PCs are the virtually identical MS-DOS and PC-DOS. These operating systems are fairly rudimentary and uncomplicated, designed to allow one user to use one program at a time on one computer. If you want to use several programs at a time on a single computer, or if several users want to use a single computer simultaneously, some other operating system would usually be more appropriate.

OS/2, a more powerful OS, is also available specifically for PCs. OS/2 supports multiple programs running on a single computer, a feature called *multitasking*. For example, when using OS/2, you could start a communications program to send a database to another computer. While the database is being sent, you can start your word-processing program and do work—the file transfer will continue in the background.

VMS is the most popular operating system for computers manufactured by Digital Equipment Corporation (DEC). VMS is designed for multi-user operation because DEC computers are multi-user. VMS is available for all of DEC's minicomputers; thus any software that runs on one DEC minicomputer can (in principle) run on all DEC minicomputers.

37

IBM minicomputers and mainframes use several operating systems. Many IBM minicomputer and mainframe users have been unpleasantly surprised to find that upgrading their systems requires *replacing* them with brand-new hardware and software. IBM is working to improve this situation with unified system standards, such as SNA (Systems Network Architecture) and SAA (Systems Application Architecture).

UNIX is another OS that is particularly interesting in that it is available on many different computers, ranging from PCs to mainframes. The wide availability of UNIX allows users to employ the same applications on all of these computers. UNIX is both multi-user and multitasking, which gives it great power and flexibility. Unfortunately, as is true with much in the computer world, along with power and flexibility comes complexity. This combination of features makes UNIX popular among programmers, but less popular with computer end users. Several organizations are working on ways to make UNIX more palatable (easier to use) to end users.

≡ THE NETWORK OPERATING SYSTEM

The three-layer model is a reasonable model of how a stand-alone computer operates. However, adding a network to a stand-alone computer adds new complexities.

The first step in attaching a stand-alone PC to a network is to add the hardware (a network interface card) that allows the PC to physically attach to the rest of the network. This additional network hardware, in turn, requires an addition to the operating system to direct its use by the application. This OS addition is the network operating system (NOS).

As we mentioned in Chapter 5, creating a network adds new functionality and flexibility to stand-alone PCs. However, it must continue to work with the same applications as did the stand-alone computer. This requirement is complicated by the fact that some functions that were previously stand-alone, such as reading from or writing to a file, might become network functions.

To illustrate this situation, let's look again at the example of how an application program reads a piece of data from a disk drive. In our earlier example, drive F: was a local disk drive. Suppose that on our networked PC, disk drive F: is now a shared network drive, accessed via the network hardware. When our same application program commands the operating system to read the eighty-seventh piece of data from drive F:, how will the OS and NOS determine which among them is to perform the function?

The answer lies in a new layer, called the **redirector**. Figure 7-5 shows how our new NOS and redirector pieces fit into our computer model. The function of the redirector is to intercept all commands sent from the application to the OS/NOS layer. The redirector determines if the request pertains to network or local hardware, and routes it to the NOS or OS, respectively. Any information returned from the hardware is passed through the redirector to the application.

Notice again that each of the four layers is a black box. It is defined purely by the inputs it receives and the outputs it produces in response to those inputs. *How* the layer does its job is not of concern to the other layers.

**FIGURE
7-5**

4-layer
networked
computer
model

Application Software	
Redirector	
Operating System	Network Operating System
Local Hardware	Network Hardware

**FIGURE
7-6**

The
7-layer
OSI
reference
model of a
networked
computer

Application
Presentation
Session
Transport
Network
Data Link
Physical

☰ THE OPEN SYSTEM INTERCONNECTION (OSI) SEVEN-LAYER MODEL

The two-, three-, and four-layer models we developed earlier all describe a computer in different levels of detail. In 1983, the International Standards Organization (ISO) approved a universal model that describes, in great detail, how the network functions of a computer ought to be organized into separate black boxes. It is called the Reference Model for Open Systems Interconnection, or the **OSI model**. The OSI model has seven layers, each of which may communicate only with the layers immediately above and below it. Each layer is defined by its inputs and outputs, and thus is a black box. A diagram of the OSI model is shown in Figure 7-6.

The primary goal in establishing a reference model is to permit communication among different computers from different manufacturers running different operating systems—as long as each system conforms to the OSI model. Also, in principal, equivalent layers from different manufacturers should be able to be substituted for each other.

The OSI model is extremely complex and subtle, requiring a fair amount of study before it becomes useful. Because OSI has become such a widely-heard buzzword (buzzacronym?), here is a brief explanation of the OSI layers.

Taken together, the layers of the OSI model are intended to ensure that data is transferred between computers in a timely and accurate manner. Individually, each OSI layer is responsible for a specific task. Let's take a closer look at how all of the layers work together. We'll start from Layer 7, the Application Layer, and work our way down.

7 As in our previous models, the Application Layer consists of the software we are using, such as a word processing, spreadsheet, or graphics program. When a computer is sending data over the network, the data starts at the Application Layer and works its way down to the Physical Layer (Layer 1), where it is placed onto the transmission medium.

6 The Presentation Layer is similar to the Operating System defined earlier. The Presentation Layer contains an extensive set of common functions that application programs can use.

5 The Session Layer is responsible for setting up and maintaining the connection between the user and the network. For example, login and logout are the responsibility of the Session Layer.

4 The job of the Transport Layer is to determine the most effective way for data to be sent to the intended recipient.

3 The Network Layer determines the routing of the message. This is generally of greater importance on wide-area networks than on local-area networks. The Network Layer is also responsible for breaking messages

received from the Transport Layer into packets of a size appropriate to the network (see Chapter 10 for more information on packets).

2 The Data Link Layer is responsible for ensuring that data sent over the Physical Layer remains free of errors. It does this by adding error detection information to each packet. The recipient of the packet will analyze this information to determine if the packet has errors. If it does, it will be sent again.

1 The Physical Layer is responsible for actually putting the packets onto the communications media, typically wire, fiber-optic cable, or satellite.

Our descriptions of the OSI model so far have concentrated on how the layers function when a computer is *sending* a message. When a message is received by a computer, it is received by the Physical Layer and works its way up to the Application Layer. Each layer performs the converse operation on the incoming data as it would to outgoing data. For example, the Physical Layer receives the raw data packets, the Data Link Layer checks for errors and orders the sender to retransmit "bad" packets, the Network Layer reassembles packets into a full message, and so on.

The final result of all of this effort is that the Application Layer on the receiving computer receives the exact message sent by the Application Layer on the sending computer. All of the layers just ensure that this happens.

Network
Cabling

EIGHT

One of the goals of a network is to allow each workstation and other members of the network (collectively called **nodes**) to communicate with all of the other nodes. Presuming that we use cable of some sort as a channel for communication, we must come up with a cabling *design* that will link every microcomputer in the network to every other computer and resource in the network. Figure 8-1 shows one direct way to do this: simply attach a cable between any two nodes. This scheme will work, but it becomes very cumbersome when we connect even moderate numbers of computers. For example, a network of twenty-five computers will require the installation of 300 cables, while a network of 250 computers will require the installation of 31,125 cables.

FIGURE 8-1

A first attempt at cabling

42

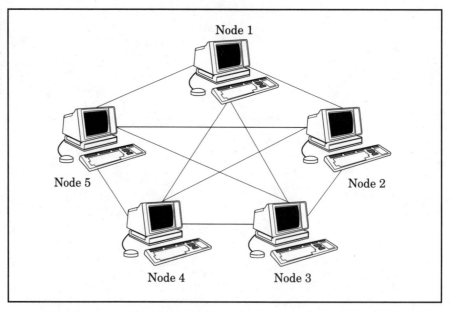

Node 1

Node 5

Node 2

Node 4

Node 3

We'd much prefer to come up with a cabling strategy that allows all computers in the network to communicate while keeping the number of cables required down to approximately one per computer.

The design of the cabling is known as the topology. There are two topologies that describe any cabling system:

- The **electrical topology** refers to which network nodes can *directly* communicate with each other.

- The **physical topology** refers to the path the cable actually follows in the physical installation.

☰ ELECTRICAL TOPOLOGY

There are two important electrical topologies: bus and ring, both pictured in Figures 8-2a and 8-2b.

Bus Electrical Topology

As we can see, the **bus electrical topology** permits a direct electrical path between any two nodes. Looking at Figure 8-2a, you can see, for example, that Node 3 can communicate directly with Nodes 1, 2, 4, and 5.

FIGURE 8-2A

Bus electrical topology

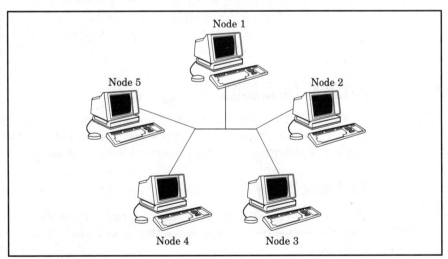

43

FIGURE 8-2B

Ring electrical topology

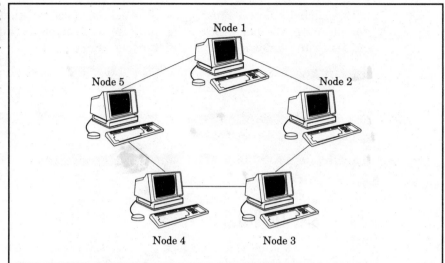

Ring Electrical Topology

The **ring electrical topology** is named for its ring shape, as seen in Figure 8-2b. In contrast to the bus electrical topology, the ring electrical topology does not provide a direct electrical path between any two nodes in the network. In a ring topology, messages must be passed down the line until they reach their destination. For Node 4 in Figure 8-2b to send data to Node 2, it must first send the message to Node 5. Node 5 passes the message to Node 1, and, finally, Node 1 passes the message to Node 2.

☰ PHYSICAL TOPOLOGIES

As mentioned before, the physical topology refers to how the cabling is actually routed. There are two important types of physical topologies: star and bus, illustrated in Figures 8-3a and 8-3b, respectively.

Star Physical Topology

The **star physical topology** gains its name from its resemblance to a star. Each node has a set of wires that goes from it to a central location, called a hub.

The big advantage of the star configuration is its resistance to failure and ease of troubleshooting. To see why this is, let's look at the case of something going wrong with the network wiring. In a star configuration, the odds are that the problem lies in one of the links between a workstation and hub. If this is the case, generally only that one workstation will be cut off from the network. Should the error somehow freeze the entire network,

**FIGURE
8-3A**

Star physical
topology

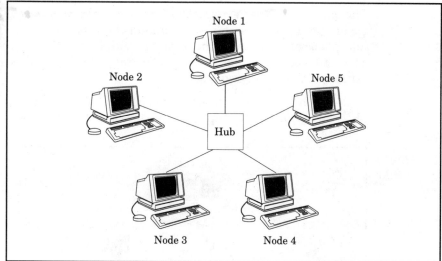

**FIGURE
8-3B**

Bus physical
topology

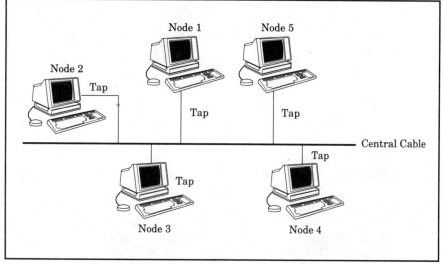

troubleshooting is relatively easy: unplug lines one at a time at the hub. As soon as the offending line is pulled, the network should spring back to life.

using ⟶ Another advantage of the star configuration is that it is the configuration in which telephone wiring is run in offices and homes. Many buildings already have unused telephone wire running through them that may be used for networking. Also, if we are already wiring a building for telephone service, it is relatively easy to add another set of wires over the same routes to use for the network.

The only real disadvantage of the star physical topology is cost. It is more expensive to run wire in a star configuration than in a bus. This may or may not be an important consideration, and should obviously be examined. The actual cost differential depends on many factors; it is best to get cost estimates before making a decision.

Both the bus and ring electrical topologies can be configured as star physical topologies. Examples of these are shown in Figures 8-4a and 8-4b.

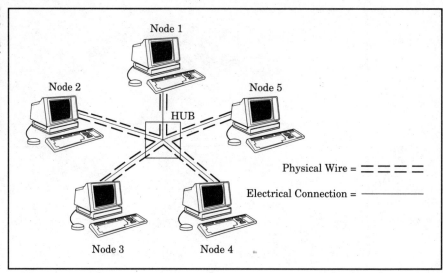

FIGURE 8-4A

Bus electrical topology, star physical topology

FIGURE 8-4B

Ring electrical topology, star physical topology

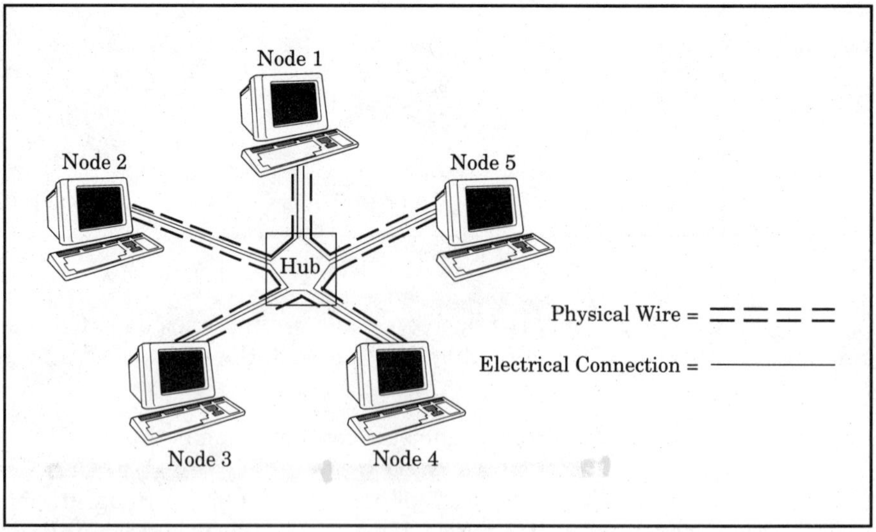

Bus Physical Topology

The other important wiring scheme is called the **bus physical topology**. The central feature of the bus physical topology is a single cable that runs throughout the facility. Each node connects to the network by connecting to the central cable. This connection from node to central cable is known as a **tap**.

Although the cost of installing cable in a bus configuration is generally lower, bus installations are somewhat more troublesome in use:

- Network hardware malfunctions are more likely to freeze the entire system.

- Troubleshooting is much more difficult. There is no central location from which we can unplug stations until things work again. We must go from station to station, unplugging and reconnecting, looking for the error. There are some sophisticated tools that make this process easier, but they are expensive and require a reasonably high level of user sophistication.

A bus physical topology only supports a bus electrical topology. Figure 8-4c illustrates the straightforward combination of bus physical and electrical topologies.

FIGURE 8-4C

Bus electrical topology, bus physical topology

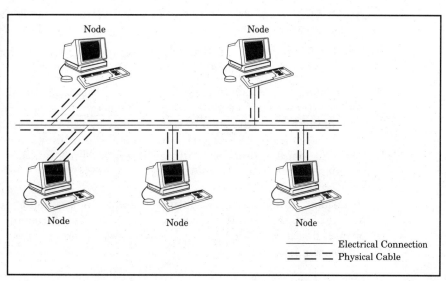

47

Types of Cabling

NINE

There are three important types of "wire" (technically known as *media*) used in LANs: twisted-pair, coaxial, and optical fiber. The first two are in general use today, while the third is becoming increasingly more common.

There are several attributes of each type of cable that are of note:

- *Cost* of the cable and associated hardware (e.g., network cards)

- *Ease of installation* can vary greatly between types of cable. Note that the ease of installation will directly affect the *cost* of installation.

- *Reliability*. While most cables are tremendously reliable, some combinations can be less than ideal.

- *Noise immunity*, which refers to the cable's ability to ignore electrical noise and interference in the environment. This is mainly a concern in facilities with many heavy-duty motors (machines, elevators, air conditioners). In severe cases, too much electrical noise leaking in may slow communications, although it probably will never scramble information. Conversely, the more immune a cable is to interfering noise, the less noise the cable itself will leak to the outside world. This may be a concern in certain situations: in health care facilities, this stray noise might upset life-support equipment. Also, the stray noise might be monitored and interpreted from a distance, which might be a consideration in security-conscious applications.

- The *speed* at which the cable can transfer data. Speed is not so important today: For example, ARCNET on fiber-optic cable will not actually work any faster than ARCNET on twisted-pair cable, despite the former medium's ability to transmit information many thousands of times faster than the latter. The speed of the cable may, however, determine the cable's future. Future networks may transfer data at higher rates than they do today, so only cable capable of supporting the faster transfer rates will be useful. Is it worth spending the extra money to ensure compatibility down the road? This can only be determined through proper network planning.

Let's examine the key attributes of the three most common types of cable.

≡ TWISTED-PAIR CABLE

Twisted-pair cable is, as might be expected, two wires intertwined (twisted around each other) over their entire length. A typical cable will contain two or more twisted pairs. Figure 9-1a shows a typical twisted-pair cable.

**FIGURE
9-1A**

Twisted-pair
cable

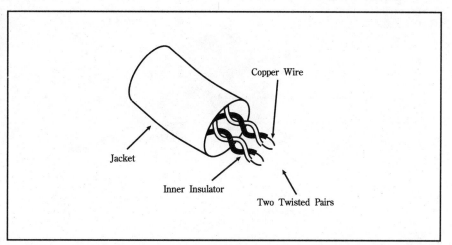

There are two types of twisted-pair cable: shielded and unshielded. Shielded twisted-pair cable has a conducting layer surrounding the twisted pairs. This conducting layer makes the cable more immune to electrical noise. Unshielded twisted pair (**UTP**) cabling lacks this shield.

All telephone companies use UTP cable to wire buildings for telephone service. Since the majority of wiring done today is done for telephone service, the same UTP cabling is often used for network connections.

49

The primary advantage of twisted-pair cable is that it is the least expensive cable to purchase and install. Because cabling costs can amount to as much as half of all network costs, this is not a trivial advantage.

On the negative side, twisted-pair cable will not support data transfer at rates as high as other types of cable. This means that at some point in the future you may want to install faster cabling—probably optical fiber. Then again, you may *never have to*.

Twisted-pair is also more susceptible to electrical noise. The noise immunity, however, is sufficient for the majority of installations.

≡ COAXIAL CABLE

Figure 9-1b shows a typical **coaxial cable**. A central wire is covered by a layer of insulation (called the dielectric). The dielectric is covered by a layer of foil or metal braid (called the shield), which is in turn covered by a final layer of insulation (called the jacket).

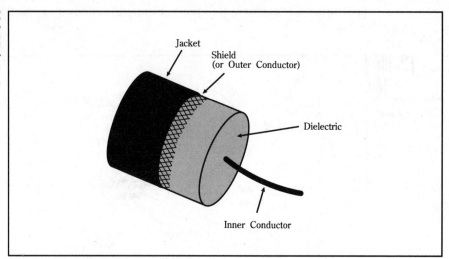

Coaxial cable falls into the middle of the cable spectrum in performance, cost, and ease of installation. It provides somewhat better electrical noise immunity than twisted-pair cable. The difference is not important for most applications, but may be significant in some circumstances.

Coaxial cable will support higher-speed data transmission rates than will twisted-pair cable. However, it is not likely that the very fast data transmission rates we will see in the future will run on coaxial cable; they will most likely be geared to faster fiber-optic cables.

FIBER-OPTIC CABLE

Twisted-pair and coaxial cable transmit electrical signals over wires; **fiber-optic cable** transmit signals using light beams. A typical fiber-optic cable is shown in Figure 9-1c. The light beam is conducted along a transparent glass or plastic fiber. This fiber has a thin coating, called cladding, which effectively acts as a mirror, ensuring that light traveling along the fiber does not leak out through the sides. The cladding is in turn surrounded by a plastic jacket whose purpose is to protect the relatively delicate fiber and cladding.

FIGURE
9-1C

Fiber-optic
cable

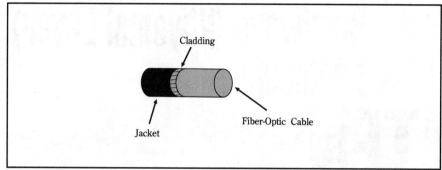

Because it transmits light rather than electricity, fiber-optic cable has extraordinary abilities compared to twisted-pair and coaxial cable.

- Fiber-optic cable is capable of supporting tremendous data transfer rates —upwards of one *billion* bps! (Refer again to Chapter 1 for more information on bps, or bits per second.)

- Fiber-optic cable is *immune* to electric interference.

- Certain types of fiber-optic cable can reliably transmit signals over extremely long distances (miles).

- There is no chance of accidental sparking, making fiber-optic cable ideal for hazardous environments.

- Because there is no metal in fiber-optic cable, it is highly resistant to corrosion, and thus suitable for hostile environments.

- A special plus for security-conscious applications is the difficulty in stealing information from fiber-optic cable. With the right equipment installed, it is virtually impossible to tap into fiber-optic cable undetected.

There are two drawbacks to fiber-optic cabling:

- Fiber-optic cabling and the hardware that supports its use are more expensive than their twisted-pair and coaxial counterparts.

- Fiber-optic cable is generally more difficult to install than twisted-pair and coaxial cable. At installation time, this difficulty translates directly into a further increase in cost.

Hardware (Physical Layer) Protocols

TEN

WHAT IS A PROTOCOL?

Whenever people or objects communicate, they must have a communication **protocol**. A protocol can be thought of as a set of rules that govern the communication. Without these rules, we would not be able to understand each other.

Morse code is an example of a protocol. Morse code allows two people to carry on a conversation using a signal, usually a tone, that can either be on (making a sound) or off (silence). In order for a Morse code conversation to take place, both parties involved must understand certain things:

- All communication is made with audible dots (•) and dashes (–).

- A dot is a sound of short duration.

- A dash is a sound that lasts for a time equal to three dots.

- Each letter of our alphabet is represented by a number of dots and dashes. (For example, A=•–, B=–•••.)

- Dots and dashes within a letter are separated by a silence that lasts for a time equal to one dot.

- Letters within a word are separated by a silence that lasts a time equal to one dash (three dots).

- Complete words are separated by a silence that lasts a time equal to two dashes.

Note that both participants in the conversation must be in complete agreement of the protocol for the communications to be successful. If, for example, one participant is under the impression that the lengths of dashes and dots are reversed from what they are supposed to be, then neither participant will be able to understand the other.

Computer networks also use protocols to communicate. These protocols are similar to Morse code in that they usually communicate using two states: voltage high and voltage low, instead of tone on and tone off.

Computer communications protocols are different from Morse code in two important respects:

- People can usually send only a few words per minute using Morse code, but computers can send hundreds of thousands of words per minute. For example, the contents of this entire book could be transferred in a few seconds.

- A computer network may need to carry on multiple "conversations" at once, but a Morse code conversation may only have two participants.

≡ PACKETS

Before we proceed with our descriptions of how the protocols operate, we should be aware of a fundamental unit of data with which all LAN protocols work: the **packet**. A packet consists of two basic parts:

1. The data that is being sent.

2. A **header**, which identifies the node to which this data is addressed or intended.

A packet is generally of a certain specific size, say, 100 characters. If an entire message to be sent is smaller than the packet size, then the rest of the packet is filled out with "dummy" characters to reach the packet size. If, on the other hand, a total message is too large to fit in one packet, it is split into several packets that are sent one at a time, then reassembled back to their original form by the recipient computer.

In this chapter, we'll examine the three most popular communications protocols for LANs: Ethernet, Token Ring, and ARCNET. All three of these protocols are known as baseband protocols, meaning that only one packet may be sent over a cable at a time.

53

≡ ETHERNET

Ethernet was developed by Xerox Corporation, and has been adopted by many companies, including Digital Equipment Corporation (DEC). DEC uses Ethernet as the basis of its DECnet network architecture. Note that this does not necessarily mean that different vendor's versions of Ethernet can coexist on the same network—they often cannot, unless you use special equipment. However, computers using DECnet, Ethernet, ARCNET,

Token Ring, or practically any other hardware protocol can communicate via bridges and gateways, as discussed in Chapter 6.

Ethernet Theory of Operation

Ethernet utilizes the bus electrical topology. Each node on the network has its own address (i.e., node number), which is set in the Ethernet hardware.

Figures 10-1a through 10-1c illustrate the operation of a typical Ethernet network. In Figure 10-1a, we see all of the Ethernet nodes "listening" to the network cable, waiting for a node to **broadcast** (send) a packet of information.

**FIGURE
10-1A**

All nodes
listening

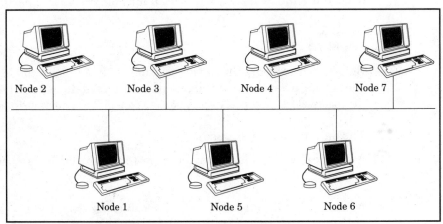

**FIGURE
10-1B**

All nodes
start
receiving
from Node 2

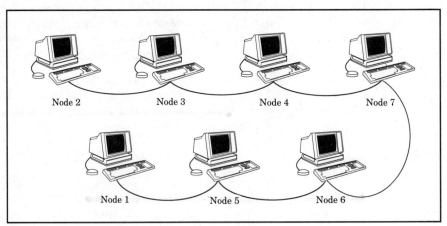

**FIGURE
10-1C**

Node 6
receives
packet from
Node 2

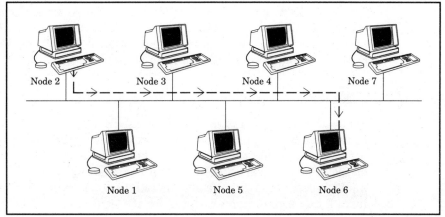

In Figure 10-1b, Node 2 broadcasts a packet. Since the cabling is a bus electrical topology, every node in the network receives this packet. Each node looks at the header to determine the intended destination of the packet.

Those nodes that are not meant to receive the packet ignore the rest of the packet (i.e., the data). The one node that *is* intended to receive the packet, in this case Node 6, listens to the entire packet (Figure 10-1c), separates the data from the header information, and acts on that data.

Once the packet is received, the network goes back to its waiting state, as in Figure 10-1a, until another packet is sent.

This procedure is straightforward, and works well until we get two or more nodes that wish to broadcast at the same time.

Let's first consider the case where Node 5 wishes to broadcast while the broadcast to Node 6 is still in progress. Node 5 must simply wait until Node 6 has received its entire packet. Once Node 5 senses that the cable is available, it may begin to broadcast its packet.

Taking this discussion a step further, let's suppose that both Nodes 1 and 5 want to broadcast a packet while Node 6's broadcast is in progress. Nodes 1 and 5 both wait for Node 6's broadcast to end. Nodes 1 and 5 will simultaneously sense that the cable is free and start to broadcast. Unfortunately, only one packet may be sent over a cable at one time, and so a **collision** will result from the two packets being simultaneously broadcast. The Ethernet hardware will sense this collision, and all broadcasts will halt. The Ethernet nodes that caused the collision will wait a short time, then will return to listening for a free cable and rebroadcast the packet. The amount of time the node waits is random—if it were the same for each node, collisions would recur continuously.

The basic Ethernet strategy of multiple nodes sharing the same cable, waiting for cable to be available before broadcasting a packet, and halting transmission if a collision is detected is known as **CSMA/CD** for Carrier Sense Multiple Access with Collision Detection.

Using Ethernet

Ethernet was originally designed for use in a bus physical topology. The central cable was a thick coaxial cable, with short twisted-pair taps along its length for each node. Generically known as **Thick Ethernet** (because of the thick central cable) installations, these are commonly found in minicomputer and mainframe installations. A typical Thick Ethernet installation is diagrammed in Figure 10-2a.

FIGURE 10-2A

Typical thick Ethernet network

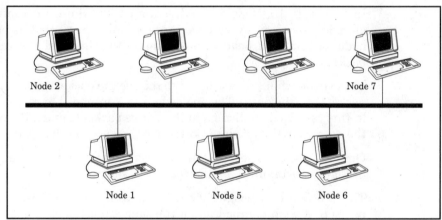

FIGURE 10-2B

Typical thin Ethernet network

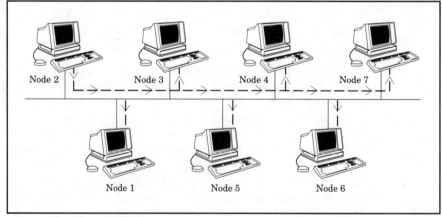

Microcomputer networks typically use a simpler, inexpensive Ethernet configuration known as **Thin Ethernet** or **Cheapernet**. Thin Ethernet refers to the use of thinner coaxial cable. A typical Thin Ethernet installation is diagrammed in Figure 10-2b. Note that there is not a separate cable for each tap—the Thin Ethernet central cable actually runs right to each workstation.

Ethernet can also use twisted-pair cable in bus or star physical topologies, and fiber-optic cable in a star physical topology. These configurations require specialized hardware.

≡ TOKEN RING

Token Ring was designed by IBM, and as such, is *IBM's* baseband network hardware of choice. This is not to say that IBM PCs must use Token Ring networks, or that non-IBM PCs cannot use Token Ring: IBM PCs and compatibles may use whichever hardware protocol is determined to best fit the application. Ethernet, Token Ring, ARCNET, and other types of network hardware may be used in the IBM PC and its compatibles.

Token Ring Theory of Operation

Token Ring networks use a ring electrical topology. Consequently, each node on the network may only directly communicate with the two nodes next to it.

The word *token* in the Token Ring name comes from the use of a small piece of data (actually a special packet) on the ring, called a **token**. There is typically one token on the network at one time. Whichever node possesses the token may send data to another node.

Figures 10-3a through 10-3f illustrate the operation of a Token Ring network. Node 1 starts with the token. Node 1 has no data to send, so the token is passed to Node 2 (Figure 10-3a).

FIGURE 10-3A

Node 1 has nothing to send— passes token to Node 2

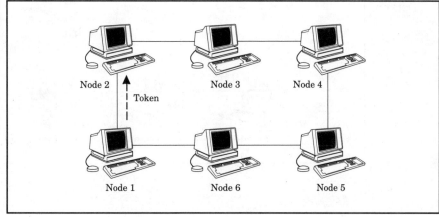

**FIGURE
10-3B**

Node 2 has
nothing to
send—
passes
token to
Node 3

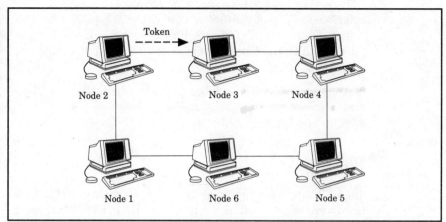

**FIGURE
10-3C**

Node 3 has
data to
send—
takes token,
sends data

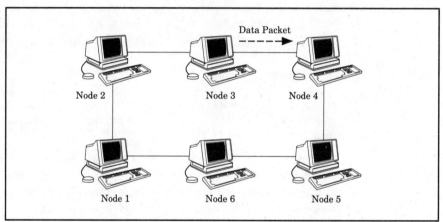

**FIGURE
10-3D**

Data not
intended for
Node 4, so
passed on
to Node 5

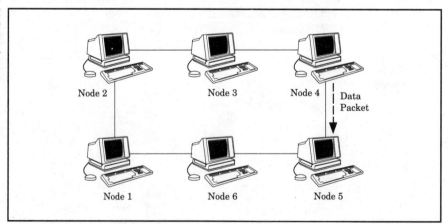

FIGURE
10-3E

Node 1
(intended
receiver)
receives
data packet
—returns
confirmation
to Node 3

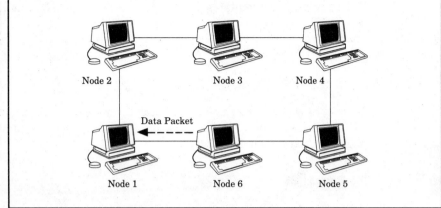

FIGURE
10-3F

Node 3
passes
token to
Node 4

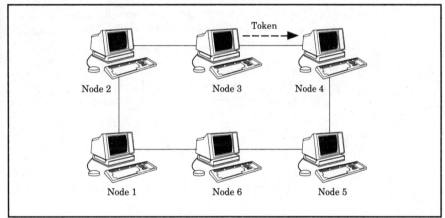

Node 2 also has no data to send, so the token is passed to Node 3 (Figure 10-3b). Node 3 has a packet to send to Node 1, so Node 3:

1. takes the token off the network

2. sends the new packet to Node 4 (Figure 10-3c).

Node 4 examines the header of the packet to see if the data is meant for it—it is not, and so it is passed to Node 5 (Figure 10-3d). Node 5 similarly examines the packet and forwards it to Node 6, which in turn forwards it to Node 1 (Figure 10-3e). The packet *is* addressed to Node 1, so Node 1:

1. takes the data off of the network

2. generates a packet (addressed to the original sender, Node 3) on the network that indicates that Node 1 has received its packet.

59

The new packet circulates back to Node 3. When Node 3 receives this notification packet, it:

1 removes it from circulation

2 sends the token on to Node 4 (Figure 10-3f).

Node 4, now possessing the token, may send a packet or pass the token on down the line. This process of passing the token and broadcasting data packets continues indefinitely.

Using Token Ring

Token Ring uses a star physical topology (refer to Figure 8-4b to see how this is done). Figure 10-4 illustrates a typical Token Ring installation. The hub in a Token Ring installation is known as a Multistation Access Unit, or MAU. Each node is cabled to a jack on the MAU. Multiple MAUs can be connected to expand the network into a distributed star.

IBM specifies that nodes be connected to MAUs with special shielded twisted-pair cabling. However, unshielded twisted pair (UTP), coaxial, and fiber-optic cables may all be used, with the appropriate special hardware.

≡ ARCNET

ARCNET was developed by Datapoint Corporation. Introduced in 1977, it is one of the most popular hardware protocols for PC LANs.

ARCNET Theory of Operation

The operating principles of ARCNET lie between those of Ethernet and Token Ring. Like Ethernet, ARCNET uses a bus electrical topology. Like Token Ring, ARCNET utilizes a token to determine who gets to broadcast. Because ARCNET employs a token passed over a bus electrical topology, it is sometimes referred to as a token bus protocol.

FIGURE 10-4

Typical token-ring installation

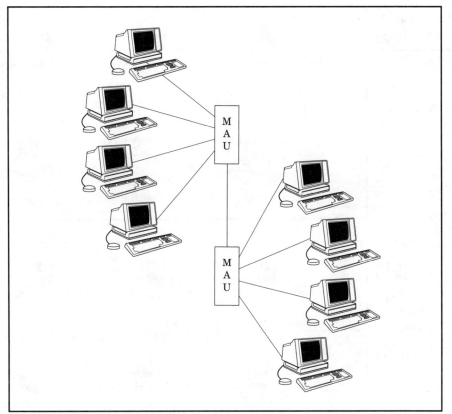

FIGURE 10-5A

Node 1 has nothing to send— passes token to Node 2

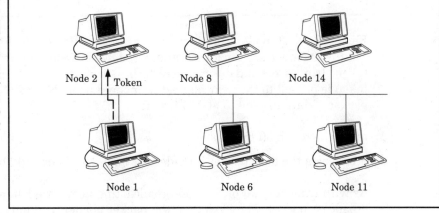

**FIGURE
10-5B**

Node 2 has
data to
send—
takes token,
sends data
packet to
Node 14.

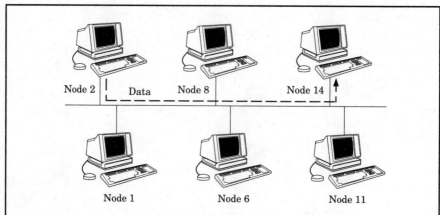

**FIGURE
10-5C**

Token
passed to
next-highest
node
(Node 6)

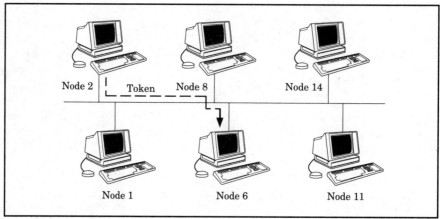

Each ARCNET node is assigned an address (number) in hardware. In Figure 10-5a, we see the lowest numbered node, Node 1, starting with the token. It does not have a message to broadcast to another node, so the token is passed to the next highest numbered node, Node 2. Node 2 has a packet of data to send to node 14, so it:

1. takes the token off the bus

2. broadcasts the data packet intended for node 14 (Figure 10-5b).

As with Ethernet, all of the non-broadcasting nodes are listening to each broadcast packet. They examine the packet header, and only the node to which the packet is addressed, Node 14 in this instance, receives the data portion.

The packet having been sent, Node 2 sends the token to the next highest numbered node, Node 6 (Figure 10-5c). Node 6 now has the option of either passing the token to the next highest-numbered node, or broadcasting a message packet.

The token continues to pass from node to node until it reaches the highest numbered node. The token then returns to the lowest-numbered node and starts working its way back up again.

Using ARCNET

ARCNET is extremely flexible: Its bus electrical topology may be implemented in a star physical topology, using either UTP, coaxial, or fiber-optic cable, and a bus physical topology using either UTP or coaxial cable.

A typical ARCNET installation is pictured in Figure 10-6. This installation is interesting in that it uses a combination of topologies and cable types. Combining topologies can be useful in some situations to best exploit the various advantages of different configurations.

**FIGURE
10-6**

Typical
ARCNET
installation

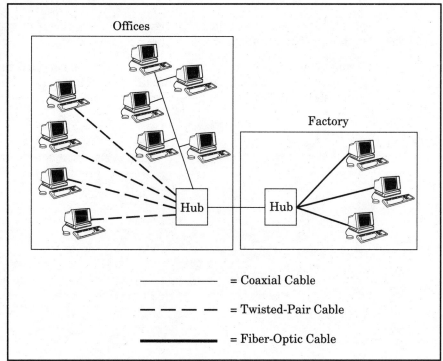

Offices

Factory

Hub

Hub

——————— = Coaxial Cable

— — — — = Twisted-Pair Cable

━━━━━━━ = Fiber-Optic Cable

Which is Fastest?

The question most often asked about hardware protocols is, "Which is fastest?" Ethernet, which transmits at 10 MBPS should in theory be the fastest, followed by 4 MBPS Token Ring, and 2.5 MBPS ARCNET.

In actual tests, however, all protocols end up transmitting information at almost the same speed. This indicates that the network hardware is not the bottleneck for communications. In other words, the network can usually send data faster than the applications can supply data to send.

The final result is that no hardware protocol is measurably slower than any other in any sort of real-word conditions. The choice of protocol should be based on flexibility, reliability, and maintainability, rather than speed.

In the case of Figure 10-6, we have a manufacturing company with two basic areas, office and manufacturing. The office area is relatively free of electrical noise, and thus is a good candidate for twisted-pair cable installation. The factory floor, by contrast, is filled with arc welders and heavy machining equipment, all of which spew a great deal of electrical noise, making fiber-optic cable the best cable choice. Adding to this mix, the previous tenants left a coaxial cable in a bus physical topology from their ARCNET network, which had connected some of the offices. Rather than compromise on one cable and topology, the company used the best cable for the appropriate situation. The old ARCNET coaxial bus was reused wherever it existed. The offices not serviced by the coaxial bus were cabled with twisted-pair cable in a star physical topology. Finally, the factory floor was cabled with fiber-optic cable, again in a star physical topology.

While combining physical topologies is a straightforward process using ARCNET, it is usually more difficult to realize with other hardware protocols, usually requiring specialized, expensive equipment if it can be done at all.

Internetworking

ELEVEN

Our discussion of networking, so far, has centered around the linking of PCs in a local-area network. There are times, however, when we would like to share resources among different *types* of computers. For example, we may want our PCs to be able to access a large database which resides on a mainframe computer. Or perhaps we would like our PCs to share the tremendous processing ability of a supercomputer. These capabilities fall under the area known as internetworking. Broadly defined, internetworking refers to the capability of substantially different networks of computers to interact with each other.

There are many degrees of internetworking, and many ways to achieve internetworking capabilities. In this chapter, we look at some of the more common internetworking capabilities.

≡ TERMINAL EMULATION

At the simplest level of internetworking, a member of one network has the ability to temporarily become a member of another network. Suppose that we would like our PC to be able to access a sales database in the mainframe computer. The most straightforward way to achieve this goal would be to outfit the PC with:

1. hardware that allows the PC to attach to the mainframe network

2. software that causes the PC to act like a terminal on the mainframe network

In Figure 11-1a, we see an installation where four PCs have been attached to a mainframe by this process. The simple terminal emulation process has the advantage of simplicity, but there are shortcomings. The most obvious inconvenience is that we must install special software and hardware in each computer that is to have the ability to link into the mainframe. Suppose we have 250 PCs that may occasionally require the use of the sales database on the mainframe. The cost of implementing this system by installing hardware in 250 computers may be prohibitive.

FIGURE 11-1A

Terminal emulation —direct connection

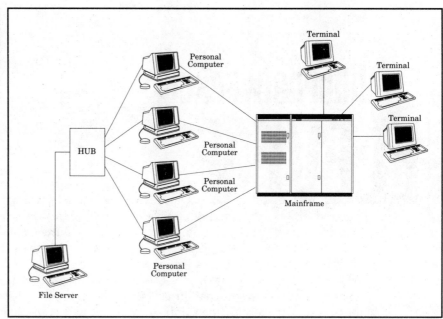

FIGURE 11-1B

Terminal emulation —gateway

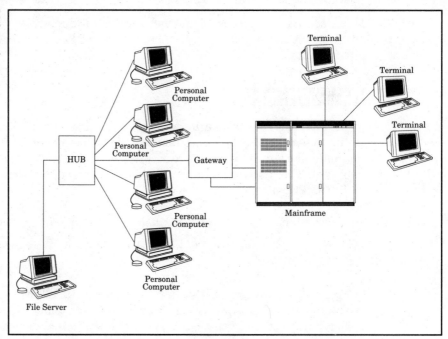

≡ NETWORK GATEWAY

In Figure 11-1b, we see the same four PCs linked to a mainframe via a network gateway. Each of the four PCs may use terminal emulation software (shared over the network, of course) to access the mainframe via the gateway. The process of an individual PC (or terminal) using the mainframe is known as a **session**. The number of sessions a gateway will support is equal to the number of PCs on the network that may *simultaneously* access the mainframe.

Compared to simple terminal emulation, a gateway system may provide many PCs with access to another network at a moderate cost. The disadvantage is that only a limited number of users may have access at a given time. Given these factors, gateways are generally most useful for PC networks that need only infrequent access to the mainframe.

≡ INTEGRATION OF INTERNETWORK RESOURCES

Now that our PCs can physically communicate with the mainframe, the second barrier to overcome is the inability to *integrate* the functions of the mainframe and the PC. Simple terminal emulation allows a PC to act as a PC, or as a mainframe terminal, but not as both. This is a serious limitation. Suppose we want to analyze our sales data, which resides on the mainframe, in a PC spreadsheet program. If we are using only the most basic level of terminal emulation, we can put the PC into terminal mode, use the mainframe to print the sales data, put the PC back into PC mode, and reenter, *by hand*, the data into the PC application. This procedure may be acceptable if only a small amount of data is involved, but is usually unacceptable for transferring large quantities of data. Beyond the amount of work involved, there is the possibility some data will be incorrectly transferred, leading to erroneous results.

We need a way to *electronically* move the data between mainframe and PC in order to eliminate the slow and tedious human intervention process. There are several ways of doing this.

The most fundamental way is to employ a utility that captures text as it goes to the PC screen while in terminal emulation mode. The captured text is placed into a PC file. After returning to PC mode, the text is read into the final PC application, in this case the spreadsheet. If the captured information is not in a form that can be readily used by the PC application (as is often the case) it may be edited using a word processor or text editor.

A more convenient procedure is to have a software package, either on the mainframe or PC, that can *directly* read the information from the mainframe and place it into a PC file in a form that is ready to use. Organizations often design custom software to accomplish this when there is data that must be moved on a regular basis.

Suppose a large clothing manufacturer performs accounting using a mainframe computer. Once a week, the accounts receivable department would like to send out reminders to those customers who are behind in their payments. The company's computer department designs a program that extracts from the mainframe the name, address, phone number, account number, overdue balance, and time overdue for each past due account and places it on the accounts payable PC LAN file server. The custom program also translates the mainframe data into a form that may be read by the PC-based word processing program. It is now a trivial matter for accounts payable to have its word processing program automatically prepare reminder notices for all overdue accounts.

The greatest degree of integration and convenience is found with applications that can directly access the mainframe's data as seamlessly as the PC data. For example, while using our spreadsheet on the PC to predict revenue growth, we could directly obtain sales data from the mainframe. From the user's point of view, it should be equally easy to use mainframe resources or LAN resources.

Wide-Area Networking

TWELVE

Local-area networks permit computers to share information over relatively short distances, several thousand feet at most. It is often desirable to share information over longer distances, say, over several miles or even across continents. Networks of this size are called **wide-area networks** (**WANs**). Here are some examples of needs that can be met by implementing a wide-area network:

- A hardware distributor has several warehouses across the country. To quote delivery times, any salesperson should be able to determine the inventory of any item at any warehouse while taking an order from a customer.

- A multinational oil company wishes to be able to send interoffice electronic mail to all of its branches worldwide.

- An environmental monitoring experiment requires that many remote PC-based air-sampling devices be scattered throughout an area of several hundred square miles. Every device takes a reading once each minute. Each day, a central computer downloads (reads) the collected data for analysis.

- A nationwide chain of clothing stores has a PC-based cash register in each location. At the close of business each day, the day's sales information is sent to a computer in the central office in Chicago, where it is analyzed to keep track of cash flow, inventory, and buying trends.

A typical WAN is pictured in Figure 12-1.

The distinguishing feature of wide-area networks is that information must travel over distances that are too great to be easily spanned by a cable. We must therefore find other ways of sending our information.

FIGURE 12-1

Typical WAN

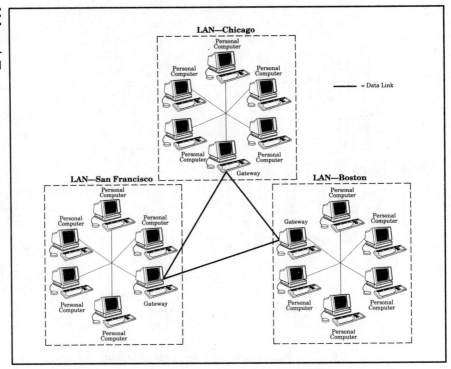

There are two basic rules in wide-area networking:

1. The longer the data link, the more it will cost to install and maintain. This is analogous to paying more for longer distance phone calls.

2. The more data that must be sent per unit of time, the more the data link will cost to install and maintain.

Most often, we do not have a say in deciding the length of the data link; we are simply given the job of moving information between, say, the New York and Montreal offices. Thus, *the main task in designing a WAN is to decrease the amount of data that must be sent over long distances.*

There are many ways to minimize data; one common way is to use codes. For example, instead of describing a desk as an "oak desk, 30 inches tall by 56 inches wide by 28 inches deep with four drawers, two of them 22 inches by 7 inches, two of them 22 inches by 13 inches," we could simply assign the code DO103 or something similar. As long as we all know what the code DO103 means, we can refer to the desk by the far shorter code rather than the complete description.

We can also decrease the amount of data to be sent by being clever in determining which information must actually be sent. Suppose we have a large inventory database of 15,000 items at each of twenty-six warehouses.

On an average day, we sell and replenish stock on only 200 different items per warehouse. At the close of each business day, we'd like to update the master inventory file on the corporate headquarters' main computer. We have two options for doing this. We could either:

1. Send the complete current inventory of each warehouse to the main computer, for a total of 15,000 items X 26 warehouses = 390,000 pieces of information to be transferred.

2. Send just the changes that have been made in each warehouse's inventory. If only 200 items change inventory level at a typical warehouse on an average day, then we only need to send 200 items X 26 warehouses = 5,200 pieces of information—a 99 percent decrease in the amount of information to be sent, and thus, a decrease in the cost of sending it.

Let's look at some of the ways we can send data over long distances.

≡ VOICE-GRADE TELEPHONE LINES

We are all familiar with the telephone system. It is a worldwide network that allows us to carry on spoken conversations with other people all over the world. The telephone system is so common, so reliable, and so easy to use that we often take it for granted.

The telephone system was originally conceived for voice communications. For this reason, standard telephone lines are often referred to as voice-grade lines. While voice-grade lines are *designed* for vocal communications, they may also be used for communicating computer data. Unfortunately, digital computer transmissions may not generally be used *directly* over standard telephone lines: as we saw in Chapter 1, voice information is analog, and thus telephone lines were designed to transmit analog signals. So a device called a modem (an acronym of MOdulator/DEModulator) is used to translate the signals for transmission over voice-grade telephone lines. Figure 12-2 shows how modems are used with computers and telephones to effect data communications. The modem is, in effect, a specialized digital-to-analog and analog-to-digital converter.

71

FIGURE 12-2

Modem operation

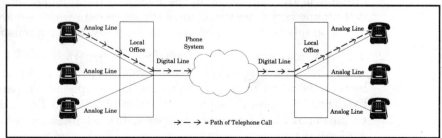

In operation, a computer sends data to the modem, which is translated to a sequence of audible tones (modulated) that are transmitted over the telephone. The receiving modem converts the modulated data back to data that the computer can use (demodulation). Note that virtually all modems can either send or receive data.

Like network hardware, modems adhere to certain protocols, and both modems participating in a communications session must adhere to the same protocol. Protocols differ primarily in the speed at which they can transfer data. Protocols exist for speeds of 300; 1,200; 2,400; 9,600; and 19,200 bps. The protocols for 300, 1,200, and 2,400 bps are fairly standard. Unfortunately there are several protocols each for 9,600 and 19,200 bps, and certain other rates that are emerging, so you must make certain that both communicating modems are using the same protocol.

To get a relative idea of the speed of modem communication, we can convert bps to characters per second by dividing by eight (there are eight bits per character). Even the fastest modem, at 19,200 bps can send only about 2,400 characters (about one standard printed page of text) each second. An Ethernet link, for comparison, can send several hundred pages per second. One page per second may be fine for sending a short document, but sending a 15 Megabyte database at that speed will take close to *two hours*.

Despite the slow transfer rates, there are many advantages that favor the use of voice-grade telephone lines, if the speed is not critical. As mentioned before, the telephone system is widespread, reliable, and easy to use. Telephones are also a relatively inexpensive way to send data over long distances.

There are two types of voice-grade telephone services of interest for use in WANs:

1. Dial-up service refers to the voice-grade telephone service with which we are all familiar. To use a dial-up line, we enter (dial) the series of pulses or tones that represent the telephone number of the site we wish to communicate. The recipient's phone rings, her modem picks up the call (the phone is answered), completing the connection. The telephone company bills the initiator of the call based on the length of the call. The advantage of a dial-up line is that we can change the location to which we are communicating simply by hanging up and dialing a new phone number.

2. A leased line is a special telephone line, generally used for computer communication, that runs between two *fixed* points. A leased line cannot be rerouted as easily as a dial-up line. The telephone company charges a fixed monthly rate for unlimited use of the leased line, with the cost proportional to the distance it spans. Leased lines are economical for applications where remote sites must regularly communicate. For infrequent communications, dial-up lines are usually more economical.

☰ LEASED DATA LINES

Special high-speed data lines, called leased data lines, are also available through various telephone carriers, such as AT&T, MCI, and US Sprint, which take advantage of existing capabilities built into the telephone system. To see how, let's look at the path of a typical telephone call.

Figure 12-3 shows the route of a typical telephone call. When a normal telephone call is placed, the signal (voice or data) leaving the premises is analog (see Chapter 1). This analog signal travels, via a twisted-pair cable, to the local telephone office. At the local telephone office, the analog signal is converted to a 64,000-bps digital signal. Several of these digital signals are multiplexed (combined) into one digital signal, which is sent to the rest of the telephone system's network over high-speed digital lines at data rates of up to 565.148 million bps. The digitized conversation is further routed through the system, until it gets to the branch office nearest its destination. Here it is demultiplexed (separated from the other digital signals), converted back to an analog signal, and sent, via twisted pair, to the destination telephone.

FIGURE 12-3

Typical phone call route

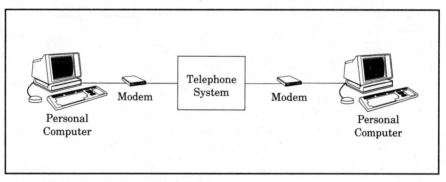

If the digital lines could be extended from the branch offices to the end users, we could have a direct high-speed digital connection from one end to the other. This can, in fact, be done. The phone company can install a special digital data line, known as a leased data line between any two points. The cost of this service depends on the distance and the maximum capacity (bps) of the connection.

73

Note that the telephone system is pictured as a "cloud" in Figure 12-3. A cloud is the networking equivalent of the electrical engineer's black box, as discussed in Chapter 7. In reality, the telephone system is an extraordinarily complex structure that can route telephone calls through a series of electrical and optical cables, satellites, and computers to ensure that they reach their destination in a time so short it is almost imperceptible to humans.

≡ PUBLIC X.25 NETWORKS

As computers sprang up around the world, the international telecommunications community realized it would be valuable to define a WAN digital communications protocol that would permit any two computers on earth to communicate with each other. This standard is known as **X.25**.

X.25 communications usually take place over public-data networks (PDNs). PDNs include Tymnet and Telenet. Once a computer has access to a public-data network, it may communicate with any other computer on the public network.

An example of how three LANs can form a WAN by using X.25 is seen in Figure 12-4. Here we see a WAN that might be installed by a national department store chain. Note that except for the speed of communications between the LANs, the three LANs can operate together as if they were one. A PC on the Chicago office's LAN can read a database file from the San Francisco office's LAN just as easily as from its own—it will just take a little longer, due to the slower speed of X.25 links as compared to LAN communications.

FIGURE 12-4

WAN (X.25)

74

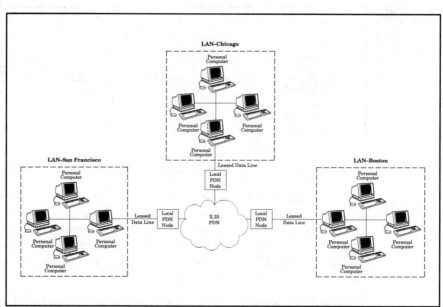

The speed of X.25 links is determined by the method used to connect to the local public data network node. A modem may be used with normal voice-grade telephone lines, which, as we've seen, will limit communications to 19,200 bps. For higher data transfer rates, a relatively short leased data line can be used to connect to the local public data network node.

From The Folks Who Brought You OSI. . .

Standardization of computer communications must be a good thing, as there are so many committees and organizations to generate standards. The standardization groups, generally known by their acronyms, include the ISO, ANSI, CCITT, ECMA, NBS, and EIA.

The king of all standards is the OSI, as described in Chapter 7. The OSI model was developed by the **International Organization for Standardization**, or **ISO** (after the acronym of the French translation). The American National Standards Institute (ANSI) is the official United States representative to ISO.

The Consultive Committee for International Telephone and Telegraph (CCITT, again, after the French) is another influential committee. CCITT standards are known as the X standards, as they all start with an X: X.25, X.400, X.500, and so forth. (By the way, the . in the X standards is pronounced "dot," as in "X dot twenty five" or "X dot four hundred."

The institute of Electrical and Electronic Engineers (IEEE) is best known for its 802 committee, which is striving to define the common local-area network standards. The best known 802 committee standard is 802.3, which describes Ethernet.

INTEGRATED SERVICES DIGITAL NETWORK (ISDN)

Just as X.25 is the data communications standard of the present, ISDN promises to be the standard for the communications network of the future. ISDN is to data communications as the telephone system is to voice communications. In fact, *ISDN will become the telephone system*.

The intent of ISDN is to implement a computer data network whose span will be the same as that of the telephone system. Computers at any location will be able to access each other and communicate without the use of modems, as easily as we currently communicate by telephone.

Besides the elimination of the modem, the advantage of ISDN is the speed of data transfer that it supports: up to 144,000 bps. This is about seven times faster than the fastest modems operating on standard telephone lines. This increase in speed, coupled with ISDN's low projected cost, may make WANs that transfer large quantities of data far more economical, and thus, far more common.

75

ISDN is designed to actually *replace* today's voice-grade telephone system. ISDN telephones convert human speech into computer data and forward it over the ISDN lines. The receiving ISDN telephone reconstructs the computer data into human speech.

Note that implementing ISDN is not quite as complex a process as it might seem: ISDN can use the same digital infrastructure that the present telephone system uses. The only major change is that the local lines, those running from telephone to branch office, must be converted to digital data lines.

≡ X.400 ELECTRONIC MAIL

An important function of a WAN is to support electronic mail (E-mail) to remote locations. **X.400** is a standard that defines the form the mail will take while in transit. Thus, the actual user interface (front end) function is left to the designer of the E-mail software. Two or more software packages may function quite differently from an end user's point of view, but if they all send and receive messages in X.400 format, they may all operate with each other.

≡ ELECTRONIC BULLETIN BOARD SYSTEMS (BBS'S)

The most common WANs for PCs are electronic bulletin board systems, or BBS's. As their name indicates, BBS's are analogous to the old cork bulletin boards. Users may "visit" the BBS and leave messages, files, programs, or other information for other BBS users. Visiting a BBS is done via modem.

BBS's are extremely popular—nobody keeps a strict count, but there are probably several thousand across the country at any one time. Many companies have set up BBS's to keep in contact with employees at home or on the road. Other companies have BBS's to keep in touch with their customers, using the BBS to answer questions and distribute updated files and information. In addition, many individuals set up BBS's simply for the fun of running one.

A typical visit starts by dialing the BBS using a communications program on a PC. After communications are established, the user is asked for his or her name and password. The BBS will now typically search and display any messages that other users have posted for the user.

The user now has a choice of three major areas to visit.

- The *Messages* area where messages can be left for specific users, general information posted for all to read, or questions asked of the BBS users in general. Most BBS's split the messages area into many subgroups dealing with specific topics, ranging from networking to cooking to poetry.

- The *Files* section, where users can find a large number of programs and data files that may be of interest. These files are usually either freeware (free software), shareware (software that may be freely shared and tried, but must be paid for if the user keeps it after trying it), and demonstrations of commercial software. Users can also leave files if they have something to share with other BBS users.

- The *Bulletins* section, which contains bulletins about the BBS itself: information on how to use it, new services, etc.

Depending on the design, more than one caller may use a BBS at a time. Some BBS's tend to attract local users, while some have an international following.

Some of the larger BBS's, such as CompuServe, may offer many services in addition to the ones mentioned above. In particular, they may offer information services, such as news, weather forecasts, and so forth. One of my favorite CompuServe services is Magazine Database, which permits me to search through back issues of over 200 magazines for articles on any topics that interest me. I can also book an airline flight, hotel and rental car with the EAASY SABRE feature.

Application Software and Networks

THIRTEEN

≡ STAND-ALONE SOFTWARE

Most of the software written for PCs was originally intended for use on a single, stand-alone PC. PC networks are designed with this in mind, and will add capabilities that are generally *transparent* to the application software. For example, as we saw in Chapter 8, the redirector and network operating system software in each workstation take care of "tricking" the application into thinking that the network resources are local resources. As far as the stand-alone application program can tell, it is just accessing local drives. It doesn't know (or care) that some of these drives are actually shared over the network.

Network transparency is useful, to a degree, because it allows us to implement networks and use the same software that we have grown accustomed to using on stand-alone computers. As we see in the following sections, transparency may also cause problems, as it may allow users to "step on each other's toes" when sharing data.

≡ NETWORK-AWARE SOFTWARE

The inability of stand-alone software to realize that it is sharing resources may occasionally cause difficulty. For example, let's suppose User A opens a document for editing. While User A is making changes, User B opens the same document for editing. User A eventually saves the document under the same name, and user B soon does the same. Whose version of the document will be stored on the network?

This depends on the application software. If the word processor being used is not network-aware, then the software will blindly save each copy, and the second version saved under the same name will overwrite the first. Consequently, User A's revisions will be lost.

File Locking

File locking is the simplest solution to this problem. File locking allows only the first open copy of a file to be altered. The network keeps track of who is working with which file. If a second or subsequent user attempts to use a file, they may read it, but they may not alter it.

Let's replay our example with a word processor that supports file locking. User A starts the word processor and opens a file for editing. The application checks to see if any other users have opened the file. They haven't, so User A may open and edit it at will. User B now opens the same file. The application checks with the network and sees that someone else is using the file, and User B is warned by the application that the file is in use. She may look at the file and make changes, but she cannot save those changes under the original file name—the altered file must be saved under a new file name. This ensures that all changes are saved, albeit in different files.

File locking is particularly useful for applications such as word processing, where *entire files* are being changed by a single person at a time. This is as compared to a database where, typically, only *one easily separated piece of information* (say, one person's insurance policy information) is being used at a time.

Note that some programs, running on some NOS's, will automatically effect file locking. No other users will be permitted to open a file while it is in use by a user.

Record Locking

Let's consider the use of a large shared database on a network. In contrast to a word processing application, a database application often *requires* that multiple users be able to simultaneously update the *same file*. For example, all telephone sales personnel for a mail-order catalog company should be able to access and change the inventory file at the same time.

79

File locking would only allow one user at a time to have full access to the inventory file. Other users would not be able to alter the file until the user with access exits the file. This could lead to quite a logjam if we have 100 sales personnel simultaneously taking orders.

A better solution for this situation is record locking, which locks individual items in a file only while the item is in use. For example, if one salesperson is updating the quantity of insulated coffee mugs in stock, another salesperson may update the number of electric espresso makers in stock. However, two salespeople may not simultaneously update the number of insulated coffee mugs. If a second salesperson tries to update this information while the first salesperson is still in the process, the second salesperson will be told that he must wait until the first salesperson is finished.

≡ NETWORK-EXPLOITING SOFTWARE

Network-aware software is aware of the network's presence, and works with the network only to make certain that accidents and unpleasant surprises do not occur. The next category of software on the evolutionary scale is network-exploiting software. This type of software uses the network's resources and capabilities to implement new and better functions. Some examples of network exploiting software are:

- electronic mail
- programs that allow network users to electronically "chat" with each other using their keyboards and monitors

≡ GROUPWARE

Groupware is a new and exciting class of network-exploiting software that addresses the needs of groups of people in organizations. One example of a groupware application is scheduling programs. Keeping track of the schedules of all the people in an organization used to be an unpleasant chore. Trying to find a time for twenty busy executives to attend a meeting on short notice was nearly impossible, usually involving many telephone calls and great frustration for any number of executives' assistants.

Scheduling software allows each member of an organization to keep track of his own schedule. When a meeting is necessary, the scheduling software will determine when all the necessary participants will be free. One of these times may be selected, and the meeting added to each participant's calendar. (Of course, E-mail should also be sent to the participants informing them of the meeting.)

Another type of groupware application can help relieve the chaos of corporate billing processes. Many organizations, such as legal, accounting, and consulting firms, bill according to the time their staff members spend on client matters. It has traditionally been very difficult for larger firms to keep track of how much time each staff member has spent on each matter. Because client billing is the life's blood of these firms, superior ways to do this are vital. This problem is alleviated by the use of time-billing software on networked PCs. Each staff member simply tells the software when he starts working on one project, and when he stops. The computer keeps track of time spent, and all the data may be easily collected at any time to keep close track of billings.

A third type of groupware is helpful in organizations where many people may be working together on documents. This software allows a document to pass from person to person for comments and revision. The software keeps track of who made what revision so that the author can know who to refer to for further clarification.

≡ CONSEQUENCES OF NETWORK/APPLICATION INTERACTION

Early PC networks often had many difficulties, usually due to problems with software that was either poorly designed or not network-aware. The situation has improved dramatically—most PC networks are now extremely reliable. So much so that they are even used in critical applications, such as banking, health care, and defense, where mistakes can be disastrous.

Terminate and Stay Resident (TSR) Software

It is worth taking a quick look at TSRs because they are often at the root of hardware and software difficulties.

Most software uses the PC's random-access memory (RAM) only when the software is active (running). TSR software is a special type of software that stays in the PC's RAM even when it is not active. The TSRs typically lie dormant in RAM, waiting for a certain event to happen, such as a certain keystroke combination. This event causes the TSR to spring to life.

An example of a TSR might be a notepad application. Suppose we receive a telephone call while using a word processor. We would like to make a note of the call on a computer notepad, a program that allows us to easily enter, store, and manage notes. If the notepad were a standard software application, we would:

- save the word processing document
- exit the word processor
- start up the notepad application
- enter the note
- exit the notepad
- restart the word processor
- reload the document
- find the place where we left off

81

If the notepad is a TSR application, we could avoid much of this inconvenience. To enter the note, we'd only:

- press a certain key combination, such as ALT-N to pop the notepad up on top of the currently operating application (in this case, the word processor)

- enter the note

- exit the notepad application. This will put us back to exactly where we left off in the word-processing application

Although TSRs simplify computer use, they can sometimes cause complications. Many network difficulties stem from TSR software. This is not to say that all TSRs cause problems—just some, under certain circumstances. In fact, the network redirector software is itself a TSR: It waits for a certain event (an application program sending a request to DOS), and springs to life in the background, determining whether to direct the request to the OS or NOS.

RAM Cram

The vast majority of PCs use the MS-DOS operating system. MS-DOS was written in the early 1980s, when microcomputers rarely had as much as 64 kilobytes (KB) of memory. The decision was made to limit the amount of memory that MS-DOS (and thus programs using it) could utilize to ten times this quantity, or 640 KB. 640 KB seemed like a lot of memory at the time—very few people ever expected microcomputers to have that much memory.

Times have changed, application software has changed (it needs more memory than it used to), but MS-DOS *hasn't* changed: it still can only utilize 640 KB. Within that space must fit the operating system, application software, and TSR software. If that isn't bad enough, the network operating system and redirector must *also* fit into this 640 KB.

Sometimes there is just not enough room to fit everything—certain applications may not have enough RAM left to operate. There are several ways to surmount this:

- Remove the TSR software while running the memory-hungry application. TSRs may take anywhere from a few hundred bytes to 100 KB or more of memory. Removing them frees a corresponding amount of memory for other software. On the down side, you cannot use a TSR when it is not installed.

- Remove the network operating system and redirector while running the application. Of course, you will lose the ability to access network resources while these are removed.

- Make use of special software that will "hide" your redirector and other TSRs in memory that is outside of DOS's 640 KB. If your PC has more than 640 KB of RAM (most newer ones do), this can free up a substantial amount of memory for applications.

Hardware and Software Conflicts

PCs are now being used in ways that were never envisioned when they were developed—networking and TSRs a case in point. There are all sorts of interesting and useful hardware and software that may be added to PCs. Unfortunately, some of these elements conflict with each other.

Most conflicts occur when more than one piece of hardware or software attempts to use the same computer resource at the same time. For example, when it springs to life, a TSR may use a certain piece of memory that the application program beneath it is already using. Exiting the TSR will cause the application to crash (stop functioning), usually with a loss of data.

In a similar fashion, two hardware devices, say, the NIC and a printer port, may each use the same memory locations. If this occurs, data intended for one of these will also go to the other, perhaps causing confusion and ultimately the temporary failure of the computer and again, a loss of data.

Hardware conflicts can usually be corrected by changing some switches on the hardware devices that tell it which resources to use. Software is usually not as flexible: often the only solution is to stop using the offending TSR or application.

Network
Design
FOURTEEN

There are three phases of network installation: planning, implementation, and ongoing support.

☰ PLANNING

The planning stage is the most overlooked element of network design—yet proper planning is crucial to the successful implementation of a network. Proper planning is necessary to ensure that the network:

- meets the present and anticipated needs and expectations of users and management
- meets budgetary guidelines
- is installed with a minimum of difficulty

Needs Analysis

The first step in planning a PC network is to identify important needs within the organization that the network can fulfill. Several major categories of needs should be examined:

- *Efficiency*. Identify ways in which the network can help employees do their jobs better and more efficiently.
- *Quality*. Consider the ways in which network applications can help provide customers with better products and services, which will in turn lead to increased revenues.

- *Decision support.* The most difficult job for an organization's management is making the decisions that can lead to prosperity—or failure. Network applications may provide management with better and more timely information on which to base these decisions.

- *Replacement of existing systems.* Many organizations are replacing existing minicomputers and mainframes with PC networks to realize increased performance and/or cost savings.

A proper needs analysis requires some effort, but when weighed against the potential benefits that a properly implemented network can achieve, it is time well spent.

The first step in the needs analysis is to hold informal informational interviews with a cross section of the people who may be affected by the network. At this point you are trying to understand:

- what people's jobs are

- what tasks are involved in doing those jobs

- what information they need to do these jobs properly

- obstacles that may impede them in the execution of their jobs

It is also helpful to inform your interviewees as to the capabilities of PC networking. Once they understand these capabilities, they may be able to take a look at their own jobs and find ways in which they can benefit from network communications. In this regard, it may be useful to schedule follow-up interviews at some point after the initial interviews to give interviewees some time to think about potential benefits.

Now it is time to start organizing the information obtained from the informal interviews. Our goal in this process is to develop a list of network requirements that will most help the organization. Be certain to look for recurring patterns, such as a lack of communication between departments or a lack of timely information. Compare the list of user's wants to the capabilities with which the network may provide them, and develop a "wish list" of capabilities for the new network.

The next part of the needs analysis is to determine which network capabilities will most benefit the organization at the least cost. Analyze each item on the wish list to determine the cost of implementing that capability vs. the benefits that it will bring. Try to develop a list of capabilities that will provide the greatest advantage at the least effort and cost. It may be helpful to distribute this list to potential users to gain feedback on the accuracy of your analysis.

System Design

The next step is to create a tentative design of the network in order to estimate its cost. A few suggestions:

- *Balance present and future needs.* Wherever you can, buy future flexibility when it only incurs a small incremental cost.

- *Search out and use existing resources.* Contact your telephone company to determine if unused cabling exists that is usable for the network.

- *There is no substitute for experience.* Make certain that someone on your design team has actually implemented a PC network. If necessary, hire an experienced consultant—a small expenditure here can save money and frustration in the end.

- *If possible, obtain all hardware, software, and services from one vendor, preferably one specializing in networking.* In this way, should problems occur in the installation, there will be only one source to contact to resolve it. Purchasing from many vendors will only lead to a lot of finger-pointing down the road.

- *Make sure estimates include costs beyond hardware and software.* Some of these, such as installation and training costs, are easier to determine. Some costs, such as temporary decreases in productivity while users get up to speed are more difficult to quantify, but can certainly impact an organization.

- *Determine the personnel required* to keep the network operable after installation. Again, an experienced networking expert can be critical in making this determination.

Cost Justification

The goal of a business is to make money. A PC network, like anything else, must contribute to that effort. The benefits of the network must increase profits enough to justify the investment in its installation. After all of the planning, estimating, and meeting, cost justification will almost always make or break the request to fund the network.

≡ IMPLEMENTATION

Network implementation is made easier by proper planning. Lack of planning, on the other hand, guarantees chaos and frustration.

It is best to phase in the network and its applications one piece at a time. In this way, when problems surface, we can easily determine their source. Start by adding an application, such as word processing, and test it. Once you are convinced it works, allow a small group of people to torture test it. Only after these tests are passed should the application be released for general use.

Try to make the installation as goof proof as possible by only giving users access to files that they need. Shared data and program files that should not be altered by end users can and should be protected by the NOS.

Physical Installation

Cable installation is the first physical step in network installation. Make certain the cabling contractor is experienced in installing the specific type of cable being used. Your own telephone company can often be a good bet for installing unshielded twisted-pair cabling.

The next step is to install a file server and a workstation. Test the communications thoroughly by using your primary applications. Add a second workstation and test the effect of two users simultaneously accessing applications. After you are certain the system is functioning properly, it is time to add the remaining workstations.

User Training

User training is critical to the success of a PC network. Initiating a comprehensive training program will ensure that network users can properly exploit network facilities and applications. Lack of training will result in:

- inefficient use of applications and facilities

- frustrated and upset users

- poor utilization of network support personnel. Instead of maintaining, troubleshooting, and adding new applications, they will spend considerable time explaining network functions to each user.

87

Here are some general suggestions for easing users' transition to the network:

- Prepare a manual that describes the use of your network system and applications. This manual may be kept on the network so frequent updates can be immediately available to all users.

- Hold formal training sessions describing the network's functions and features. This has two benefits: users will learn how to use the system, and they may also generate ideas on how the network may be used more effectively.

- Hold frequent informal sessions where users may ask questions and make suggestions, etc. This ensures that user's questions are answered, and increases the administrator's understanding of how the network is being used. Knowing how the network is used, in turn, will help in fine-tuning network procedures and adding new features and applications.

- Set up a system for training new users. Large organizations may require formal classes, while smaller organizations may opt for a more casual approach.

Network
Administration

FIFTEEN

A computer network is often regarded as a collection of hardware and software that works together to help end users perform their jobs. There is another element that is crucial to the network's functioning—network administration. The skill with which network administration is planned and executed will affect the network's operation no less than the choice of hardware and software.

Network administration comprises the tasks necessary to keep a network operating properly. In a perfect world, a network would do whatever the end users asked of it, flawlessly, twenty-four hours a day, every day of the year. In the real world, the best we can ask for is a network that performs its specified functions with few interruptions.

Among the network administration tasks are:

- keeping the network operational for all users
- educating network users as to what they can do and how they can accomplish it
- adding capabilities to the network
- fulfilling management requests
- fulfilling end-user requests
- soothing users who are frustrated when the network can't do what they'd like
- ensuring that data is backed up (copied) regularly so that it may be easily restored in the case of network failure

Often overlooked is the human relations aspect of network administration. We often forget that end users usually interact with administrators when something is not working properly, and the end user is frustrated or upset.

Beyond fixing or explaining the technical difficulty, it is vital that the administrator also be able to keep end users satisfied.

Different organizations may have different strategies for performing network administration. Smaller organizations often have a more informal approach to administration, distributing the various tasks as parts of several people's jobs. Larger organizations usually have one or more people whose jobs are dedicated to maintaining the network. Deciding *how* the administration tasks are distributed is not nearly as important as ensuring that they get done.

☰ CHANGING THE NETWORK CONFIGURATION

The only thing that is certain in this world is change. As time goes on, networks change. Managing this change to maximize network functionality and end-user satisfaction is the job of the network administrator. Several things that must be balanced when making changes to the network include:

• the changes that will be made

• the potential inconvenience to end users during the time the changes are being implemented

• the effect of these changes on how users operate their workstations

• how the changes may affect future plans for the network

☰ BACKUPS AND ARCHIVING

Q. What is the most expensive and vital part of a computer system?

A. The information it holds.

Think for a moment. We do not use computers for the sake of using computers. We use computers because they give us an unmatched ability to store and manipulate information. The computers are important, but not nearly as important as the information they hold.

No matter how well we design and maintain our network, it may fail and lose information. Actually, it is more common for users to inadvertently erase, misplace, or otherwise lose data because of their own error.

Whatever the cause of the data loss, it is critical that we be able to recover as much of the data as we can. To ensure our ability to recover data, we must make copies of our data, called **backups**, onto diskettes or other media at regular intervals. Thus, when data is lost, we may copy it back from the backup device to the network.

As we use a computer system over time, more and more information gets stored in it. After a while, the amount of information stored in the computer for quick access may become greater than we would like: the computer may run out of storage space, or the amount of information may become unwieldy to sort through and manipulate. At this point we may want to remove old or seldom-used information from the computer, but keep it in a form that allows us to easily load it back to the computer should the need arise. This process is known as **archival storage**, or archiving.

Backing up and archiving data are similar processes in that the goal of both is to make an extremely reliable and long-lasting copy of information on our computer system. In practice, archiving and backup tasks are usually performed using the same equipment.

Storage Media

The storage media refers to the actual material or mechanism that holds our backup or archive. There are many factors that may be balanced in designing a network, but there is one primary factor in choosing a backup or archive system: reliability. *The one thing we want to be certain of is that we can retrieve our data!* Because of this need for reliability, data is usually backed up or archived to magnetic tape of some sort, rather than to the magnetic hard-disk drives that are used to store data on a moment-to-moment basis on computers. While magnetic hard-disk drives are very speedy and reliable, they cannot match the reliability of slower magnetic tape systems.

Magneto-optical disk systems are also becoming important for backup use. These systems match the reliability of magnetic tapes while roughly matching the speed of magnetic fixed disks.

Storage Facilities

Taking reliability a step further, we must be careful of *where* our backups are stored. Storing backups in close proximity to the computer system (known as on-site storage) is convenient, because it is easy to store the backups and retrieve them when necessary. On-site storage also poses a danger in that a major disaster that damages our computer, such as a fire or flood, may also render our backups unusable.

In order to avert the destruction of backups by disasters, we can store our backups away from our facility (off-site) in specially designed and constructed data-storage facilities. These facilities are usually impervious to damage by all but the most severe disasters (such as war).

In practice, most organizations will opt for a combination of on-site and off-site storage to realize a compromise between convenience and security.

Full vs. Incremental Backups

Let's say we've just set up our computer system and have been entering information into our accounting program. At the end of the first day, we make a backup of all the information on the computer. Because we are copying *all* the information in the computer, this process is known as a **full backup**.

At the end of the second day, we'll want to make another backup. We could make a full backup as we did previously. Alternately, we could make a backup of *only the information that has changed since the computer was last backed up*. This is known as an **incremental backup**. The computer system keeps track of when files have changed, and the backup software may be instructed to only back up files changed since a certain time and date.

The advantage of the incremental backup is speed. If only, say, 20 percent of the information in the network has changed since the last back up, the incremental backup may be complete in as little as 20 percent of the time it takes to complete a full backup. Any files that have not changed since the last backup are on a previous backup tape.

The disadvantage of an incremental backup is that it does not contain a complete record of what was on the hard drive. To find a missing given file, we may have to go through several generations of backups.

In practice, most facilities use a combination of full and incremental backups. Fast incremental backups are performed often, perhaps daily, while full backups are performed occasionally, perhaps once a week. Doing a periodic full backup, while not theoretically necessary, ensures that we will not have to search through too many backups in the event of a damaged or lost file.

≡ TROUBLESHOOTING

A properly designed computer network will not fail very often. When it does, the ability to get it back up and running are vital to keeping a business running.

The first line of defense in troubleshooting is proper design of the network. Proper system design can help guard against network failure. In the rare event of a failure in a properly designed network, the problem may be tracked down and solved within minutes.

When a failure does occur, it is up to the network administrator to solve the problem. Because the failure may be a function of almost any element of the network, the administrator must be familiar with all aspects of the network and the ways in which it is used. It is often useful for the network administrator to be able to call on a group of users who are expert in various applications to aid in troubleshooting certain end-user problems.

Glossary of Networking Terms

analog A signal that may be varied continuously between two values. For example, an analog electrical signal on a cable could be at *any* value between 0 and 12 volts at a given time. Compare to *digital*.

application software The computer program that the user accesses. Examples of application software include word-processing, spreadsheet, and database software.

archival storage The storage of data, usually on magnetic tape, that is no longer in active use, but may be needed in the future.

ARCNET A type of hardware protocol governing communications between two or more local-area network (LAN) nodes.

backup A copy of data stored on a computer. In the event that data is lost from the computer, the backup copy will still have a recent version of the data.

baseband A communications system in which only one piece of information may be transferred over a link at a time. Compare to *broadband*.

baud A baud is equal to the number of signal changes per second. This is often the same quantity as bits per second (bps), but not always. For example, 300 bps modems run at 300 baud. All 19,200 bps modems use each signal transition to represent *more than one bit*, so their baud rate is substantially lower than 19,200.

bit Abbreviation of Binary digIT. The most basic unit of digital computing, a bit can be in only one of two states, 0 or 1.

bridge A device connecting two networks, which may or may not be using the same hardware protocol (i.e., Ethernet or ARCNET), but must be using the same network operating system. Compare with *gateway*.

broadband A communications system in which multiple messages may be simultaneously transferred over a path. Compare to *baseband*.

broadcast To send information, particularly data packets, on a network.

bus physical topology A topology defined by a single central cable that passes throughout the network. All nodes connect to the network by attaching to the central cable. Compare to *star physical topology*.

bus electrical topology An electrical topology in which all nodes are electrically connected to each other. Packets broadcast by any node are received by all other nodes. Compare to ring electrical topology.

byte A grouping of eight bits. Bytes are commonly used to represent alphanumeric characters or the integers from 0 to 255.

cabling The physical medium that connects the elements of a network, enabling them to communicate.

cheapernet See *thin Ethernet*.

coaxial cable A type of electrical cable. A central wire is covered by a layer of insulation (the dielectric). The dielectric is covered by a layer of foil or metal braid (the shield), which in turn is covered by a final layer of insulation (the jacket).

collision A condition where two packets are simultaneously broadcast on a single baseband network cable.

CSMA/CD Acronym for Carrier Sense Multiple Access with Collision Detection. A communications strategy in which multiple nodes share the same baseband cable. Each node must wait for the cable to be available before broadcasting a packet. If two packets are broadcast simultaneously by accident, a collision occurs; transmission is halted, and the transmitting nodes wait a short, random period of time before restarting transmission.

dedicated Used for one purpose. For example, a dedicated file server may be used only as a file server, and not as a workstation.

database server A network resource that stores one or more databases. Compared to a file server, a database server is optimized for sharing databases.

digital A signal that can only be in one of two states, such as 0 or 5 volts. Compare to *analog*.

electrical topology Referring to the way the network elements are electrically connected. Two electrically connected nodes will always receive the same signals at the same time. Compare to *physical topology*.

E-mail See *electronic mail*.

electronic mail Messages (e.g., letters, memos, notes) sent over a network.

Ethernet A type of hardware protocol governing communications between two or more local-area network (LAN) nodes.

fault tolerance The ability to resist and recover from breakdowns and errors.

file server A network device that stores files for use by workstations. From the network user's perspective, a file server is a large, fast hard drive shared by all network users. File servers are usually micro-computers running a special program that instructs them on how to interact with the network. Minicomputers and mainframes may also be used as file servers.

fiber-optic cable Cable used for fiber-optic communications.

fiber-optic communications Fiber-optic communications use light, rather than electricity, to communicate. Compared to electrical communications, fiber-optic communications systems are typically faster, relatively immune to the environment, and more costly to implement.

full backup A backup of an entire network hard drive.

gateway A device that allows two dissimilar networks to communicate. The networks may or may not use a different hardware protocol (e.g., ARCNET, Token Ring), but will have different network operating systems.

hardware The physical parts of a computer and network.

header The first part of a packet. The header usually contains infor-mation about the type of packet and the node to which it is addressed.

hub A device that physically connects two or more cables together. The hub is the central point in the star physical topology.

incremental backup A backup of files that have changed since a previous backup.

IEEE Acronym for the Institute of Electrical and Electronic Engineers.

IEEE 802.3 The IEEE definition of Ethernet.

IEEE 802.5 The IEEE standard for Token Ring.

LAN See *local-area network*.

login The process of notifying a network that you are using a specific workstation. Login defines the start of a session.

logout The process of notifying a network that you are ending a session on a specific workstation. Logout defines the end of a session.

95

local-area network	An assemblage of computer hardware and software that enables computers to share data, software, and other resources. The computers within a LAN are separated by small distances, say, 1,000 meters or less. Compare to a wide-area network.
mainframe	A large, powerful computer that is shared by many users via terminals. Compare to *minicomputer* and *microcomputer*.
MAU	See *multistation access unit*.
microcomputer	Small, inexpensive computers. Microcomputers are usually utilized by one person at a time (i.e., they are not multi-user). Compare to *mainframe* and *minicomputer*.
minicomputer	A medium-sized computer that is shared by man users via terminals. Compare to *mainframe* and *microcomputer*.
multistation access unit (MAU)	A Token Ring hub.
network interface card (NIC)	A printed circuit board that plugs into a computer; contains the circuitry and connectors that permit the computer to connect to the network.
network operating system (NOS)	The software that works with the network hardware to enable communications among the elements of the network.
network supervisor	The person in charge of a network.
NIC	See *network interface card*.
node	Any device that may send and/or receive data over a network. Nodes include workstations, servers, bridges, and gateways.
NOS	See *network operating system*.
OS	See *operating system*.
OSI model	The Open Systems Interconnection Model, an internationally recognized seven-layer model of how a network should operate.
operating system (OS)	A layer of software that mediates between the application software and computer hardware.
packet	A basic unit of network communications; all communications over a network involve the sending and receiving of packets of information.

peer-to-peer resource sharing	The ability to share the resources of network workstations, not just dedicated servers.
PC	Generic term for the IBM PC and compatible microcomputers.
physical topology	Referring to the physical paths followed by the network cabling. Compare to *electrical topology*.
printer redirection	The ability to send printing to shared network printers.
print server	A device that coordinates the shared printer resources of a network.
protocol	A set of rules that govern communications. For communications to be successful, all parties must use the same protocol.
queue	A waiting line in which each item follows the other.
redirector	A layer of software that intercepts application software calls to the operating system. The calls are analyzed and sent to the local operating system or network operating system as appropriate.
repeater	A device that merely boosts a signal and passes it on. Repeaters are sometimes used over long cable lengths to ensure that signals do not get too weak as they traverse the cable.
ring electrical topology	A design in which each network node is electrically connected only to two other nodes.
server	A network member that provides some service to the network workstations.
session	A continuous period of time a users spends connected to a network. A session starts at login and ends at logout.
software	A set of instructions (a program) that tells a computer what to do.
star physical topology	An arrangement in which each network node is connected to a central hub via a cable.
tap	A physical connection. Specifically, a short twisted-pair cable connection between a node and a thick Ethernet central cable.
terminal	A device that attaches to a multi-user computer. A terminal has a keyboard for entering information into the computer, and a monitor for displaying information from the computer. A terminal has no computing power of its own.
thick Ethernet	Type of Ethernet typically found in minicomputer installations. A thick coaxial cable runs throughout the installation. Nodes connect to this central cable by short twisted-pair cable taps.

97

thin Ethernet	Type of Ethernet typically found in microcomputer installations. A thin coaxial cable runs directly to each node.
token	A special type of packet used to arbitrate communications.
token ring	A type of hardware protocol governing communications between two or more local-area-network nodes.
topology	See *electrical topology* and *physical topology*.
twisted-pair cable	A cable containing one or more pairs of intertwined wires. It may or may not be shielded with an additional conductive layer surrounding the wires.
UTP	Unshielded twisted-pair cable. See *twisted-pair cable*.
WAN	See *wide-area network*.
wide-area network	Provides computer communications over large distances. Wide-area networks often tie together groups of LANs separated by large geographic distances. Compare to *local-area network*.
workstation	A computer used to execute software and access a LAN. Workstations are the computers that users use directly.
X.25	A hardware protocol typically used for wide-area networks.
X.400	A protocol for the exchange of electronic mail.
X.500	A protocol that governs the naming of users and resources in wide-area networks.

Index